CUADERNO

2

An Intermediate

Workbook for

Grammar and

Communication

Pg. 198

Ronni L. Gordon, Ph.D.
David M. Stillman, Ph.D.

WHAT?

National Textbook Company
a division of NTC/CONTEMPORARY PUBLISHING GROUP
Lincolnwood, Illinois USA

Editorial Development: Mediatheque Publishers Services, Philadelphia, Pennsylvania

ISBN: 0-8442-7926-9

CONTENTS

PREFACE

Cuaderno 2: An Intermediate Workbook for Grammar and Communication is designed to provide intermediate students of Spanish with the tools they need to consolidate what they have learned, to review and practice key topics covered in the second year, and to lay a solid foundation for more advanced study. Organized in 19 chapters, *Cuaderno 2* presents concise, well-organized **grammar explanations** with clear, practical examples that reflect everyday usage. The **exercises** in *Cuaderno 2* provide ample review of basic structures, especially verb forms, and offer varied practice in the patterns presented in most second-year Spanish textbooks. These exercises reinforce communicative goals by offering students contextualized practice of structures that helps them build accuracy and confidence. **Vocabulary** items have been chosen to review and expand upon those presented in second-year basal textbooks. When an exercise uses words and expressions not commonly found in second-year textbooks, the words are presented and defined in a **vocabulary box** preceding the exercise.

Cuaderno 2 highlights important features of the Spanish-speaking world in **culture boxes** that appear in every chapter and that help create an authentic context for a particular exercise. Some of the features of the Spanish-speaking world presented in the culture boxes are history, geography, climate, vacations, food, economy, politics, music, art, and the press. Progressing from structured to self-expression exercises, every chapter of *Cuaderno 2* provides **Preguntas personales** and **Composición** activities to encourage learners to use the grammatical structures and vocabulary they have studied to express their own ideas.

Students will find that working through *Cuaderno 2* is both productive and enjoyable because of the easy-to-follow format, the ample space provided to write answers, the clear and practical presentation of grammar, and the open, inviting design. Teachers will appreciate the flexible organization of *Cuaderno 2*, which allows them to select chapters in any order to reinforce the grammar points they are presenting in their classes. The unique integration of all its features makes *Cuaderno 2* an engaging, user-friendly workbook that motivates learners to communicate and helps build a real sense of accomplishment as students progress in their study of Spanish. This student-centered, communicative approach makes *Cuaderno 2* the perfect companion for every second-year textbook.

The Present Tense: Regular Verbs; Stem-Changing Verbs; Verbs with Spelling Changes; Hace + Expression of Time + que + Verb

CHAPTER

1

I. The Present Tense: Regular Verbs

■ All Spanish verbs belong to one of three different classes, or *conjugations.* The one they belong to is determined by the ending of the infinitive, which is the verb form that ends in **-ar, -er,** or **-ir.** Study the following conjugations:–

LLEGAR *TO ARRIVE*

	singular		plural	
first person	yo	llego	nosotros/-as	llegamos
second person	tú	llegas	vosotros/-as	llegáis
third person	él		ellos	
	ella	llega	ellas	llegan
	usted		ustedes	

APRENDER *TO LEARN*

	singular		plural	
first person	yo	aprendo	nosotros/-as	aprendemos
second person	tú	aprendes	vosotros/-as	aprendéis
third person	él		ellos	
	ella	aprende	ellas	aprenden
	usted		ustedes	

VIVIR *TO LIVE*

	singular		plural	
first person	yo	vivo	nosotros/-as	vivimos
second person	tú	vives	vosotros/-as	vivís
third person	él		ellos	
	ella	vive	ellas	viven
	usted		ustedes	

■ The present-tense forms of Spanish verbs express the English simple present *(you listen)* and the English present progressive *(you're listening):*

Escuchamos música clásica.   *We listen to classical music. / We're listening to classical music.*

■ The present tense can refer to the future if another element of the sentence expresses future time:

Isabel vive en Barcelona el año próximo.   *Isabel will be living in Barcelona next year.*

Los estudiantes entregan el informe el jueves.   *The students are handing in the report on Thursday.*

- The first-person singular and the first-person plural of the present tense can be used to ask for instructions:

  ¿Abro el paquete ahora?   *Shall I open the package now?*

  ¿Viajamos en tren?   *Shall we travel by train?*

Notes:

1. Subject pronouns are used less frequently in Spanish than in English because the verb endings show who the performer of the action is. Subject pronouns are used to contrast or emphasize the subject of the verb:

   —**¿Dónde viven** *Uds.***?**   *"Where do you live?"*
   —*Yo* **vivo en el centro, pero** *él* **vive en las afueras.**   *"I live in the city, but he lives in the suburbs."*

2. Spanish has four forms for *you*. They show politeness and number. **Vosotros/vosotras,** the informal plural, is used only in Spain. Therefore, in Latin American Spanish, there are three forms for *you*: an informal singular form, **tú;** a formal singular form, **usted;** and one plural form, **ustedes,** that is used to address any group of two or more people.

3. **Usted** and **ustedes** are abbreviated **Ud.** and **Uds.** in Latin America, and often **Vd.** and **Vds.** in Spain.

- Questions can be formed in Spanish by inverting (changing the order of) the subject and the verb or merely by changing intonation:

  Uds. enseñan español.

  ¿Enseñan Uds. español? }
  ¿Uds. enseñan español? }   *Do you teach Spanish?*

A. ¿Qué pasa en la escuela secundaria? Write sentences with the correct present-tense form of the verbs given to describe what is happening at school today.

Modelo   los alumnos / escuchar casetes de español
➤ Los alumnos escuchan casetes de español.

[handwritten notes in margin:]
☺ +8
A+
① Los alumnos sacan buenas notas.
② Maria soluciona problemas.
③ Nosotros tomamos apuntes.
④ Maria y Lupe trabajan en parejas.

La vida escolar (School life)

sacar buenas notas *to get good grades*	**tomar apuntes** *to take notes*
solucionar problemas *to solve problems*	**trabajar en parejas** *to work in pairs*

---

1. yo / leer el libro de texto

   Yo leo el libro de texto

2. tú / solucionar unos problemas de física

   Tú solucionas unos problemas de fiesta

3. Cecilia / aprender unas fechas de memoria

Cecilia aprende unas fechas de memoria

4. los estudiantes / trabajar en parejas

Los estudiantes trabajan en parejas

5. nosotros / discutir unos temas políticos

Nosotros discutimos unos temas políticos

6. Uds. / tomar apuntes

Uds. toman apuntes

7. el profesor Marqués / enseñar literatura norteamericana

El profesor Marqués enseña literatura norteamericana

8. vosotros / sacar buenas notas en los exámenes

Vosotros sacáis buenas notas en los exámenes

B. ¡Qué malcriados! *(What brats!)* Pilar works part-time at a nursery school. Find out what her days are like by writing sentences with the correct present-tense form of the verbs given.

Modelo   los padres / dejar a sus hijitos en el preescolar
➤ Los padres dejan a sus hijitos en el preescolar.

En el preescolar (In pre-school)	
armar un lío *to raise a fuss, to cause trouble*	**medio muerto** *half-dead*
el (colegio) preescolar *nursery school*	**mimado** *spoiled*
	pegar *to hit*

Los niños arman un lío en preescolar. La niña pega el ból. La comida fue mimado. Los niños son medio muerto.

1. Pedrito / gritar

Pedrito grita

2. los niñitos mimados / armar un lío

Los niñitos mimados arman un lío

3. tú, Sarita, / llorar todo el día

Tú y Sarita lloráis todo el día

➤➤➤➤➤

4. Florecita y Joselito / molestar a sus compañeros

Florecita y Joselito molestan a sus compañeros

5. Elenita / correr por el comedor

Elenita corre por el comedor

6. Uds., muchachitos, / romper los juguetes

Uds. y muchachitos rompen los juguetes

7. Luisito / pegar a los otros niños

Luisito pega a los otros niños

8. ¡los maestros y yo / terminar el día medio muertos!

¡los maestros y yo terminamos el día medio muertos!

Note: The diminutive ending -**ito** suggests smallness or endearment: **Joselito, Sarita, muchachitos.**

C. **Un apartamento para cuatro amigas.** You and three friends are sharing an apartment while you attend summer school. Tell why you get along as roommates. Write the correct present-tense form of the verbs.

Modelo   nosotras / buscar casa ➤ Nosotras buscamos casa.

1. mis tres amigas y yo / alquilar *(to rent)* un apartamento

Mis tres amigas y yo alquilamos un apartamento

2. yo / compartir un cuarto con Beatriz

Yo compato un cuarto con Beatrix

3. Julia y Tere / desear dormir en el segundo dormitorio

Julia y Tere desean dormir (dormen) en el segundo dormitorio

4. Tere y yo / cocinar y quitar la mesa

Tere y yo cocinamos y quitamos la mesa

5. Julia / lavar y secar los platos

Julia lava y seca los platos

6. Beatriz / sacudir el polvo y barrer los pisos

Beatriz sacude el polvo y barre los pisos

7. todas nosotras / comprar comida para una fiesta

Todas nosotras compramos comida para una fiesta

−1 ✗
8. nuestros amigos / comer y celebrar con nosotras

Nuestros amigos comemos y celebramos con nosotras
                    en   *en*

D. Benjamín está enfermo. Describe Benjamín's day at home with a cold. Write the correct present-tense form of the verbs in parentheses.

El resfriado (The cold)

estornudar *to sneeze*	**el pañuelo de papel** *tissue*
guardar cama *to stay in bed*	**la sopa de gallina** *chicken soup*
el jarabe para la tos *cough syrup*	**toser** *to cough*

Benjamín no _asiste_ (1. asistir) a sus clases hoy porque está resfriado. Sus papás no lo _dejan_ (2. dejar) ir al colegio. Su mamá _cree_ (3. creer) que Benjamín _debe_ (4. deber) guardar cama porque el chico _estornuda_ (5. estornudar) y _tose_ (6. toser) mucho. Su papá _sale_ (7. salir) a la farmacia donde _compra_ (8. comprar) unas cosas para su hijito. Él _regresa_ (9. regresar) a casa con aspirinas, pañuelos de papel y jarabe para la tos. La abuela de Benjamín _prepara_ (10. preparar) una sopa de gallina para su nieto. Benjamín _come_ (11. comer) sopa y pan tostado y _bebe_ (12. beber) té. El chico _lee_ (13. leer) un libro y _mira_ (14. mirar) la tele.

1) Benjamin estornuda el pañuelo de papel
                    en
2) Benjamin guada cama y come la sopa de gallina
3) Benjamin tose y bebe el jarabe para la tos

II. The Present Tense: Stem-Changing Verbs

Stem-changing verbs that end in -ar and -er

- Many regular verbs in Spanish have changes in the vowels of the stem in certain persons of the present tense. A change of **e ≻ ie** or **o ≻ ue** occurs in all persons, except the **nosotros** and **vosotros** forms. Study the following conjugations:

EMPEZAR (e ≻ ie) *TO BEGIN*

	singular	plural
first person	empiezo	empezamos
second person	empiezas	empezáis
third person	empieza	empiezan

QUERER (e ≻ ie) *TO WANT*

	singular	plural
first person	quiero	queremos
second person	quieres	queréis
third person	quiere	quieren

ENCONTRAR (o ≻ ue) *TO FIND*

	singular	plural
first person	encuentro	encontramos
second person	encuentras	encontráis
third person	encuentra	encuentran

PODER (o ≻ ue) *CAN, TO BE ABLE*

	singular	plural
first person	puedo	podemos
second person	puedes	podéis
third person	puede	pueden

- Some common **e ≻ ie** stem-changing verbs:

cerrar *to close*	**pensar** *to think*
comenzar *to begin*	**perder** *to lose; to miss (train, etc.); to waste (time)*
empezar *to begin*	
entender *to understand*	**querer decir** *to mean*
nevar *to snow (used only in third-person singular:* **Nieva.** *It's snowing.)*	**recomendar** *to recommend*

Notes:

1. **Pensar** is used with the preposition **en** to mean *to think about* something:

—¿En qué piensas?   *"What are you thinking about?"*
—Pienso en las vacaciones.   *"I'm thinking about (my) vacation."*

2. **Pensar** is used with the preposition **de** to mean *to have an opinion about something:*

—¿Qué piensas de esta   *"What do you think about this*
    computadora?   *computer?"*
—Creo que funciona muy bien.   *"I think it works very well."*

■ Some common **o ➤ ue** stem-changing verbs:

almorzar *to have lunch*

aprobar *to pass (an exam)* approve

contar *to count; to tell*

costar *to cost*

demostrar *to show; to prove*

devolver *to return/give something back*

doler *(used with indirect object pronoun) to hurt, to ache*

jugar (u ➤ ue) a *to play (a sport or game)*

llover *to rain (used only in third-person singular:* **Llueve.** *It's raining.)*

mostrar *to show*

probar *to try; to taste*

recordar *to remember*

resolver *to solve*

volver *to return; to go/come back*

Stem-changing verbs that end in *-ir*

■ Some **-ir** verbs change **e** to **i** in the stem in all persons, except the **nosotros** and **vosotros** forms. Study the following conjugation:

PEDIR (e ➤ i) *TO ASK FOR; TO ORDER*

	singular	plural
first person	pido	pedimos
second person	pides	pedís
third person	pide	piden

■ Some common **e ➤ i** stem-changing **-ir** verbs:

conseguir *to get, to acquire; to manage to (with infinitive)*

repetir *to repeat; to have a second helping of food*

seguir *to follow, to continue*

servir *to serve*

Note: The verbs **seguir** and **conseguir** also have spelling changes (see section III of this chapter).

■ Some **-ir** verbs change **e** to **ie** in the stem in all persons, except the **nosotros** and **vosotros** forms. Study the following conjugation:

PREFERIR (e ➤ ie) *TO PREFER*

	singular	plural
first person	prefiero	preferimos
second person	prefieres	preferís
third person	prefiere	prefieren

- Some common **e** ➤ **ie** stem-changing **-ir** verbs:

mentir *to lie*   **sentir** *to be sorry (with **lo**: **lo siento**)*
referir *to refer*   **sugerir** *to suggest*

- Some **-ir** verbs, such as **dormir** and **morir,** change **o** to **ue** in all persons, except the **nosotros** and **vosotros** forms. Study the following conjugation:

DORMIR (o ➤ ue) *TO SLEEP*

	singular	plural
first person	duermo	dormimos
second person	duermes	dormís
third person	duerme	duermen

E. **¡Qué flojos!** *(What lazy people!)* Nobody wants to work on getting out the next issue of the school paper. Construct sentences that express people's negative attitudes by writing the correct present-tense form of the verbs.

Modelo   Lorenzo / no querer hacer nada
➤ Lorenzo no quiere hacer nada.

Verbos (Verbs)

colaborar *to contribute; to collaborate*

contar con *to count on, to rely on*

despedir *to send away; to dismiss*

---

1. Paloma y Javier / preferir no trabajar

    Paloma y Javier prefieren no trabajar

2. tú / repetir que no tienes tiempo

    Tú repites que no tienes tiempo

3. Claudia / no poder esta semana

    Claudia no puede esta semana

4. yo / no contar con nadie

    Yo no cuento con nadie

5. Uds. / sentirlo

    Uds. siéntenlo

6. Ud. / no sugerir ningún tema

    Ud. no sugiere ningún tema

7. vosotros / no querer colaborar

Vosotros no queréis colaborar

8. nosotros / despedir a todos los periodistas

Nosotros despedimos a todos los periodistas

F. Una tarde tranquila. Tell what you and other people are doing to relax this afternoon by writing sentences with the correct present-tense form of the verbs.

Modelo   ellas / mostrar su álbum de sellos
➤ Ellas muestran su álbum de sellos.

1. Jaime y Blanca / jugar al ajedrez

Jaime y Blanca juegan al ajedrez

2. tú / contar chistes *(jokes)*

Tú cuentas chistes

3. yo / empezar una novela policíaca

Yo empiezo una novela policíaca

4. Claudia / dormir la siesta

Claudia duerme la siesta

5. nosotros / querer ver una película

Nosotros queremos ver una película

6. Uds. / merendar *(to have a snack)*

Uds. meriendan

La merienda en España

In Spain, **merendar** or **tomar la merienda** means *to have a light afternoon snack*. Whether at home or outside the home, Spaniards eat a snack around five o'clock. It might be as simple as a cup of coffee or hot chocolate with **churros madrileños** (Madrid-style doughnuts, which are long and thin and served with powdered sugar), or it might also be more substantial, including meats, cheeses, and other foods.

G. Un viaje. Tell about Juan Antonio's trip to visit his girlfriend. Fill in the correct form of the verbs in parentheses.

Día de lluvia (A rainy day)

el limpiaparabrisas *windshield wiper*
llover a cántaros *to rain hard; to rain cats and dogs*

Juan Antonio _quiere_ (1. querer) visitar a su novia Pamela.

Él _prefiere_ (2. preferir) viajar en tren, pero llega tarde a la estación

y _pierde_ (3. perder) el último tren de la mañana. Entonces,

vuelve (4. volver) a casa y sale en su coche. Muy pronto

comienza (5. comenzar) a llover. Juan Antonio pone sus

limpiaparabrisas. ¡ _llueve_ (6. llover) a cántaros! Hay mucha niebla

y Juan Antonio no _puede_ (7. poder) ver nada. Lee las instrucciones

de Pamela y _sigue_ (8. seguir) por la carretera. Juan Antonio

empieza (9. empezar) a tener hambre. Para en un restaurante

y _almuerza_ (10. almorzar). Una hora después _vuelve_

(11. volver) a la carretera. Con suerte, Juan Antonio _consigue_

(12. conseguir) ver a su novia.

III. The Present Tense: Verbs with Spelling Changes

■ Some verbs have spelling changes in the present tense. For verbs that end in -ger and -gir, the **g** changes to **j** before the vowels **o** and **a**. In the present tense, this change occurs only in the first-person singular (**yo**) form. Study the following conjugation:

ESCOGER *TO CHOOSE, TO SELECT*

	singular	plural
first person	escojo	escogemos
second person	escoges	escogéis
third person	escoge	escogen

- For verbs that end in -**guir**, the **gu** changes to **g** before the vowels **o** and **a**. In the present tense, this change occurs only in the first-person singular (**yo**) form. Note that **seguir** also has the stem change **e ➤ i**:

SEGUIR *TO FOLLOW, TO CONTINUE*

	singular	plural
first person	sigo	seguimos
second person	sigues	seguís
third person	sigue	siguen

- Verbs that end in -**uir**, excluding those ending in -**guir**, add **y** after the **u** in all forms except **nosotros** and **vosotros**. Study the following conjugation:

INCLUIR *TO INCLUDE*

	singular	plural
first person	incluyo	incluimos
second person	incluyes	incluís
third person	incluye	incluyen

- Some verbs that end in -**iar** or -**uar** stress the **i** (**í**) or the **u** (**ú**) in all forms, except **nosotros** and **vosotros,** in the present tense. Study these conjugations:

ENVIAR *TO SEND*

	singular	plural
first person	envío	enviamos
second person	envías	enviáis
third person	envía	envían

CONTINUAR *TO CONTINUE*

	singular	plural
first person	continúo	continuamos
second person	continúas	continuáis
third person	continúa	continúan

- For most verbs that end in -**cer** or -**cir**, the **c** changes to **z** before the vowels **o** and **a.** In the present tense, this change occurs only in the first-person singular (**yo**) form:

CONVENCER *TO CONVINCE*

	singular	plural
first person	convenzo	convencemos
second person	convences	convencéis
third person	convence	convencen

H. **Completa la tabla.** Complete the following chart by writing the **yo**, **nosotros**, and **Uds.** forms of each verb.

Algunos verbos	
concluir *to finish; to deduce*	**recoger** *to pick up; to gather*
esparcir *to scatter*	**vencer** *to conquer; to defeat*
huir *to flee*	

	yo	nosotros	Uds.
1. recoger	*recojo*	*recogemos*	*recogen*
2. vencer	*venzo*	*vencemos*	*vencen*
3. huir	*huyo*	*huimos*	*huyen*
4. conseguir	*consigo*	*conseguimos*	*consiguen*
5. concluir	*concluyo*	*concluimos*	*concluyen*
6. esquiar	*esquío*	*esquiamos*	*esquían*
7. continuar	*continúo*	*continuamos*	*continúan*
8. esparcir	*esparzo*	*esparcimos*	*esparcen*

IV. The Present Tense: *Hace* + Expression of Time + *que* + Verb

■ In Spanish the construction **hace** + expression of time + **que** + verb in the present tense indicates an action that began in the past and is continuing in the present. To ask how long something has been going on, the construction **¿Cuánto tiempo hace** + **que** + verb in present tense? is used. The word **tiempo** may be omitted. See these examples:

—¿Cuánto (tiempo) hace que Uds. viven en los suburbios?   *"How long have you been living in the suburbs?"*
—Hace siete años que vivimos en los suburbios.   *"We've been living in the suburbs for seven years."*

■ **Hace** + expression of time may appear at the end of the sentence:

—¿Cuánto (tiempo) hace que estudias español?   *"How long have you been studying Spanish?"*
—Estudio español hace dos años.   *"I've been studying Spanish for two years."*

I. ¿Cuánto tiempo hace que...? Write dialogues in which one person asks another how long something has been going on (**¿Cuánto tiempo hace que...?**), and the other person answers by telling how long (**Hace** + expression of time + **que** + verb in the present tense).

Modelo   tú / esperar el autobús : media hora
➤ —¿Cuánto tiempo hace que esperas el autobús?
➤ —Hace media hora que espero el autobús.

1. Diana y Luisa / limpiar su habitación : diez minutos

—¿Cuánto tiempo hace que Uds. limpian su habitación

—Hace diez minutos que limpiamos nuestro habitación

2. el televisor / no funcionar : una semana

—¿Cuánto tiempo hace que él no funciona?

—Hace una semana que no funciona

3. Ud. / enviar mensajes por correo electrónico : quince minutos

—¿Cuánto tiempo hace que ud. envia mensajes por correo electrónico

—Hace quince minutos que yo envio mensajes por correo electrónico

4. Arturo / estar en la reunión : casi dos horas

—¿Cuánto tiempo hace que ud. está en la reunión?

—Hace casi dos horas que yo estoy en la reunión

5. Uds. / almorzar : veinte minutos

—¿Cuánto tiempo hace que uds. almuerzan?

—Hace veinte minutos que almorzamos

6. tú / trabajar para el jefe de la empresa : un par de meses

—¿Cuánto tiempo hace que tú trabajas para el jefe de la empresa?

—Hace un par de meses que yo trabajo para el jefe de la empresa

J. Preguntas personales. Answer the following questions in complete Spanish sentences.

1. ¿Qué cosas haces todos los días?

What things do you do everyday?

Yo duermo y yo come todos los días

2. ¿Qué platos pides en tu restaurante favorito?

What plates do you order in your fav. restaurant?

Yo pido el burrito en La Casa Lupita

3. ¿Duermes la siesta todos los días?

Do you sleep everyday (nap)?

No, no duermo la siesta todos los días

4. ¿A qué juegos y deportes juegas?

Do you play sports?... which ones?

No juego los deportes

5. ¿Qué libros, periódicos y revistas lees?

What books or newspapers do you read?

Yo leo el Rolling Stone

6. ¿Cómo ahorras dinero? ¿Para qué lo ahorras?

How do you save money? For what do you save it for?

Yo ahorro dinero por compro poco. Yo compro la ropa

7. ¿Qué cosas haces cuando estás enfermo/enferma?

What things do you do when you're sick?

Yo duermo y yo toso cuando estoy enferma

8. ¿Cuánto hace que vives en tu pueblo o ciudad?

How long have you lived in your city?

Hace quince años que vivo en mi cuidad.

K. Composición. Write a composition of eight to ten sentences in which you describe your activities at home, at school, and at work or in extracurricular activities. Try to use as many **-ar, -er,** and **-ir** verbs as you can, including those with stem changes and spelling changes.

The Present Tense of Irregular Verbs

There are many irregular verbs in Spanish. Some are irregular in one form only; others are irregular in all forms.

■ The verbs in the following group are irregular in the first-person singular (**yo**) form in the present tense because they have an unexpected **-g-**. All the other forms are regular. Study the following conjugations:

HACER *TO DO; TO MAKE*		**PONER** *TO PUT*	
hago	hacemos	**pongo**	ponemos
haces	hacéis	pones	ponéis
hace	hacen	pone	ponen

SALIR *TO GO OUT, LEAVE*		**TRAER** *TO BRING*	
salgo	salimos	**traigo**	traemos
sales	salís	traes	traéis
sale	salen	trae	traen

CAER *TO FALL*		**VALER** *TO BE WORTH*	
caigo	caemos	**valgo**	valemos
caes	caéis	vales	valéis
cae	caen	vale	valen

Note: Verbs that are formed by adding a prefix to an irregular verb are conjugated like the irregular verb: **suponer (supongo)**, *to suppose;* **rehacer (rehago)**, *to do again, redo;* **sobresalir (sobresalgo)**, *to excel;* **extraer (extraigo)**, *to extract.*

■ The verbs **saber** *(to know)* and **caber** *(to fit)* have an irregular first-person form in the present tense. All the other forms are regular. Study their conjugations:

SABER *TO KNOW*		**CABER** *TO FIT*	
sé	sabemos	**quepo**	cabemos
sabes	sabéis	cabes	cabéis
sabe	saben	cabe	caben

■ The verb **conocer** *(to know)* also has an irregular first-person form in the present tense. Like many verbs that have a vowel before **-cer** or **-cir**, the **c** changes to **zc** before the ending **-o**:

CONOCER *TO KNOW*	
conozco	conocemos
conoces	conocéis
conoce	conocen

■ Some verbs that end in **-ecer** and **-ucir** are conjugated like **conocer**—that is, the first-person form ends in **-zco:**

-ecer	-ucir
agradecer *to thank*	**conducir** *to drive*
aparecer *to appear*	**producir** *to produce*
crecer *to grow*	**traducir** *to translate*
desaparecer *to disappear*	
establecer *to establish*	
ofrecer *to offer*	
parecer *to seem*	
pertenecer *to belong*	

■ The following verbs have an irregular **-g-** in the first-person singular form and are irregular in other forms as well:

DECIR *TO SAY, TELL*

digo	decimos
dices	decís
dice	dicen

TENER *TO HAVE*

tengo	tenemos
tienes	tenéis
tiene	tienen

VENIR *TO COME*

vengo	venimos
vienes	venís
viene	vienen

OÍR *TO HEAR*

oigo	oímos
oyes	oís
oye	oyen

Note: Verbs that are formed by adding a prefix to **tener** are conjugated like **tener: detener** *(to stop)*, **mantener** *(to maintain)*, **obtener** *(to obtain)*.

■ The present tense of the verbs **ir** *(to go)* and **dar** *(to give)* are conjugated like regular **-ar** verbs. They are irregular because the **yo** form ends in **-oy:**

IR *TO GO*

voy	vamos
vas	vais
va	van

DAR *TO GIVE*

doy	damos
das	dais
da	dan

■ The verb **ver** *(to see)* is a regular **-er** verb in the present tense, except for the **yo** form:

ser   estar

VER *TO SEE*

veo	vemos
ves	veis
ve	ven

A. ¡Hacemos ejercicio! *(We're exercising!)* Tell what these people are doing to keep fit. Use the verb **hacer** in your sentences.

Modelo   (Leti) / hacer ejercicio ➤ Hace ejercicio.

1. (tú) / hacer equitación

   Haces equitación

2. (Pedro y Sofía) / hacer ejercicios aeróbicos

   Hacen ejercicios aeróbicos

3. (yo) / hacer ciclismo

   Hago ciclismo

4. (Uds.) / hacer yoga

   Hacen yoga

5. (Consuelo y yo) / hacer gimnasia

   Hacemos gimnasia

6. (Eduardo) / hacer caminatas

   Hace caminatas

7. (vosotros) / hacer windsurfing

   Hacéis windsurfing

B. ¿Quién lo hace? Say that the answer is *I* (**yo**) for each of the following questions.

Modelo   ¿Quién da permiso? ➤ Yo doy permiso.

1. ¿Quién pone la habitación en orden?

   Yo pongo la habitación en orden

2. ¿Quién hace travesuras *(plays tricks)*?

   Yo hago travesuras

3. ¿Quién sabe la dirección?

   Yo sé la dirección

4. ¿Quién conduce al centro comercial?

   Yo conduzco al centro comercial

➤➤➤➤➤

5. ¿Quién ve televisión?

Yo veo televisión

6. ¿Quién sale al jardín botánico?

Yo salgo al jardín botánico

7. ¿Quién ofrece bombones?

Yo ofrezo bombones

8. ¿Quién trae la mochila?

Yo traigo la mochila

C. Modismos con tener. Write sentences with the appropriate form of **tener** and the words given.

Modelo   nosotros / tener razón ➤ Nosotros tenemos razón.

1. Jaime / tener mucho éxito

Jaime Tiene mucho éxito

2. los niños / tener hambre y sed

Los niños tienen hambre y sed

3. yo / tener dieciséis años

Yo tengo dieciséis años

4. Uds. / tener mucha suerte

Uds. tienen mucha suerte

5. Matilde y yo / tener prisa

Matilde y yo tenemos prisa

6. (tú) / ¿tener ganas de dar un paseo?

¿Tú tienes ganas de dar un paseo?

7. Ud. / tener sueño

Ud. tiene sueño

8. vosotros / tener miedo

Vosotros tenéis miedo

D. Van a... Tell where you and other people are going today by writing sentences with forms of the verb **ir.** Remember to use the contraction **al** when necessary.

Modelo los tíos / la iglesia ➤ Los tíos van a la iglesia.

1. José María y yo / la biblioteca

   José, María, y yo vamos a la biblioteca

2. Ud. / el almacén

   Ud. va a̶ el almacén (al)

3. yo / el banco

   Yo voy al banco

4. Uds. / el cine

   Uds. van al cine

5. Cristóbal y Marisa / el acuario

   Cristóbal y Maria van al acuario

6. tú / la florería

   Tú vas a la florería

7. el abuelo / el templo

   El abuelo va al templo

8. vosotros / la tienda de comestibles

   Vosotros vais a la tienda de comestibles

Una tienda con muchos nombres

In Spanish there are several different ways to say *grocery store*. In Spain, a grocery store is called **la tienda de comestibles, la mantequería,** or **la tienda de ultramarinos.** In other Spanish-speaking countries, a grocery store is known as **la bodega, la tienda de abarrotes, el abasto, el colmado, la pulpería,** or **el almacén.**

E. **¿De dónde vienen?** Tell where you and other people are coming from today. Write sentences with forms of the verb **venir**. Remember to use the contraction **del** when necessary.

Modelo   Roberto / el circo ➤ Roberto viene del circo.

1. tú / la playa   _Tú vienes de la playa_

2. Agustín / el veterinario   _Agustín viene del veterinario_

3. Uds. / la estación de tren   _Uds. vienen de la estación de tren_

4. yo / el teatro   _Yo vengo del teatro_

5. Susana y Ud. / la discoteca   _Susana y Ud. vienen de la discoteca_

6. nosotros / el centro   _Nosotros venimos del centro_

7. Ud. / la fábrica   _Ud. viene de la fábrica_

8. vosotras / el parque zoológico   _Vosotras venís del parque zoológico_

F. **¿Qué dicen?** Complete the following sentences by writing the correct form of the verb given in parentheses.

Modelo   PABLO: —¿Qué _traes_ (traer, tú) en la mochila?

1. RICARDO: —Yo no _veo_ (ver) a Yolanda. Sofía, ¿tú

   ves (ver) a Yolanda por aquí?

2. SOFÍA: —En realidad, Ricardo, no ~~conoce~~ _conozco_ (conocer) a Yolanda.

   Ni _sé_ (saber, yo) quién es.

3. ERNESTO: —Yo _salgo_ (salir) con mis amigos a las siete.

   Jorge, ¿_vienes_ (venir, tú) con nosotros?

4. JORGE: —Si yo ~~traigo~~ _quepo_ (caber) en el coche, claro que

   voy a (ir) con ustedes.

5. TERESA: —Cecilia, yo _pongo_ (poner) la mesa ahora.

   ¿_sabes_ (saber, tú) dónde están las servilletas?

6. CECILIA: —Yo _tengo_ (tener) las servilletas en el comedor.

   Te las _traigo_ (traer, yo) ahora mismo.

■ The irregular verbs **decir, oír, saber,** and **ver** can have sentences as objects. These sentences, called *subordinate clauses,* are linked to the verbs by the conjunction **que** *(that)*. In English, the conjunction is sometimes omitted, but it must always be included in Spanish:

Dicen que llueve.   *They say (that) it's raining.*

Veo que usan la computadora.   *I see (that) they're using the*
                                          computer.

G. En el Teatro de Bellas Artes. A group of students hopes to attend a performance of the *Ballet Folklórico de México.* Write sentences with the verbs **decir, oír, ver,** and **saber** and the subordinate clauses given.

Modelo   Carlos / saber que no quedan entradas
          ➤ Carlos sabe que no quedan entradas.

En el teatro (At the theater)	
la entrada *ticket*	**el público** *audience*
la función *performance*	**el traje regional** *regional costume*

1. yo / saber que hay muchos aficionados al ballet

   Yo sé que hay muchas aficionados al ballet

2. tú / decir que el salón es grande y hermoso

   Tú dices que el salón es grande y hermoso

3. Irene y Clara / ver que los bailarines llevan trajes regionales

   Irene y Clara ven que los bailarines llevan trajes regionales

4. Manolo y yo / oír que hay funciones los domingos por la mañana

   Manolo y yo oímos que hay funciones los domingos por la mañana

5. yo / decir que la orquesta empieza a tocar

   Yo digo que la orquesta empieza a tocar

6. Uds. / oír que el público está muy entusiasmado

   Uds. oyen que el público está muy entusiamado

El Palacio de Bellas Artes

In the heart of Mexico City is the cultural center **el Palacio de Bellas Artes.** The building, made of white marble, was designed by an Italian architect. Its construction was begun in 1900. The **Palacio** houses a concert and opera hall, **el Teatro de Bellas Artes.** It is the home of the celebrated **Ballet Folklórico de México,** which performs regional dances of Mexico every Sunday at 9:30 A.M. and 9:00 P.M., and on Wednesdays at 9:00 P.M. The hall, with a seating capacity of 3,400 people, has a magnificent stained glass curtain designed by Tiffany that is raised and lowered with each performance of the **Ballet Folklórico.** The **Palacio** also has a museum with old and contemporary paintings, prints, sculptures, and murals. Works of Rivera, Orozco, Tamayo, and Siqueiros, some of Mexico's most famous artists, are on exhibit.

H. Unas vacaciones ideales. Complete this story about an ideal vacation. Write the correct form of the verb in parentheses.

Palabras útiles (Useful words)

dar a *to face*	**los servicios** *facilities, amenities*
mientras *while*	**el telesquí** *ski lift*

Jaime y Bárbara Sotelo _tienen_ (1. tener) un mes de

vacaciones. Este año _van_ (2. ir) de vacaciones en enero. Ellos

hacen (3. hacer) un viaje a Suiza. Jaime _hace_ (4. hacer)

reservación en un hotel que queda cerca del telesquí. Los Sotelo

dicen (5. decir) que el Hotel Verbier _tiene_ (6. tener)

todos los servicios, hasta una piscina. Su habitación _da_ (7. dar)

a unas montañas cubiertas de nieve. Ellos _ven_ (8. ver) un paisaje

hermoso. Jaime _va_ (9. ir) a esquiar todos los días mientras

Bárbara _conoce_ (10. conocer) los pueblos cercanos.

I. Una amiga por correspondencia (A pen pal). Complete the following paragraph by writing the correct form of the verb in parentheses.

Yo ___tengo___ (1. tener) una amiga por correspondencia que vive en Lima. Yo le ___pone___ (2. poner) una carta una vez a la semana. Todas las cartas y tarjetas postales que Verónica me manda ya no ___cabe___ (3. caber) en mi cajita especial. Ella ___dice___ (4. decir) que ___viene___ (5. venir) a verme en el verano. Ella ___va___ (6. ir) a estar de vacaciones. Verónica no ___conoce___ (7. conocer) los Estados Unidos. Yo siempre le ___digo___ (8. decir) que mi país es maravilloso. Yo ___voy___ (9. ir) a Lima para ver a Verónica durante las vacaciones de Navidad. ¡Yo ___hago___ (10. hacer) turismo también!

J. Preguntas personales. Answer the following questions in complete Spanish sentences.

1. ¿Qué haces los fines de semana?

   ___Yo duermo y yo salgo con mis amigos___

2. ¿De qué tienes miedo?

   ___Yo tengo miedo de los rátones___

3. ¿Adónde vas hoy? ¿Cuándo vas?

   ___Yo va a escuela hoy. Yo va a las siete en la mañana___

4. ¿Das fiestas? ¿Cuándo las haces?

   ___No doy fiestas___

5. ¿A quiénes ves todos los días?

   ___Yo voy a la fiesta de Jessica todos los días___

6. ¿Qué ruidos oyes en la calle?

   ___Yo no oigo ruidos en la calle___

K. Composición. Write a composition of eight to ten sentences about a party you are giving. Tell why you are having the party, who is coming, what foods and gifts people are bringing, what you are putting on the table, and other details. Use as many irregular verbs as you can.

The Conjugated Verb + Infinitive Construction;
The Conjugated Verb + Preposition +
Infinitive Construction

I. The Conjugated Verb + Infinitive Construction

■ In the verb + infinitive construction, the conjugated verb is followed directly by the infinitive:

—Paco, ¿quieres jugar al baloncesto?	*"Paco, do you want to play basketball?"*
—Puedo jugar en la tarde. Ahora necesito estudiar.	*"I can play in the afternoon. I have to study now."*

■ Some verbs that are often followed directly by an infinitive:

conseguir (e ➢ i) *to succeed in; to manage to*	**necesitar** *to need; to have to*
deber *should, ought to*	**pensar (e ➢ ie)** *to intend to, to plan to*
decidir *to decide*	**poder (o ➢ ue)** *can, to be able to*
dejar *to let, to allow*	**preferir (e ➢ ie)** *to prefer*
desear *to want*	**querer (e ➢ ie)** *to want*
esperar *to hope; to expect; to wait*	**saber** *to know how to*

Note: See Chapter 1 to review the conjugations of stem-changing verbs in the present tense. See Chapter 2 to review **saber.**

A. Verbo + infinitivo. Practice the conjugated verb + infinitive construction. Expand each of the following sentences with the verb in parentheses.

Modelo   Javier toma el examen de biología. (necesitar)
➢ Javier necesita tomar el examen de biología.

1. Yo voy al cine. (querer)

   _____

2. Sergio encuentra su cartera. (esperar)

   _____

3. Paloma y Ud. almuerzan en la cafetería. (decidir)

   _____

4. ¿Tú no recuerdas la dirección? (poder)

   _____

5. Ud. duerme la siesta. (pensar)

_____

6. Julián y Carmen usan la computadora. (deber)

_____

7. Aurora y yo no vamos a la reunión. (conseguir)

_____

8. Vosotros venís con nosotros, ¿verdad? (desear)

_____

B. ¡Tomo una resolución! *(I'm making a resolution!)* Tell what New Year's resolutions Rosario is making. Use the verbs in parentheses to expand the sentences.

Modelo   Saco buenas notas en todas las materias. (pensar)
➤ Pienso sacar buenas notas en todas las materias.

Palabras útiles (Useful words)

hacer las paces *to make up*

la obra maestra *masterpiece*

perfeccionar *to improve, to brush up*

---

1. Perfecciono mi español. (esperar)

_____

2. Pongo mi cuarto en orden todos los días. (querer)

_____

3. Leo cien obras maestras de la literatura. (pensar)

_____

4. Hago las paces con Luisa. (querer)

_____

5. Practico el piano dos horas al día. (esperar)

_____

➤➤➤➤➤

6. Sigo los consejos de mis papás. (querer)

_____

7. Conduzco con cuidado. (pensar)

_____

8. Llevo una vida sana. (esperar)

_____

II. The Conjugated Verb + Preposition (or Other Word) + Infinitive Construction

Ir a + infinitive, *acabar de* + infinitive, *tener que* + infinitive

■ **Ir** requires the preposition **a** before the infinitive and **acabar** requires the preposition **de** before the infinitive. **Tener** and the following infinitive must be linked by the word **que.**

■ **Ir a** + infinitive means *to be going to* do something. It is used to refer to future time:

—¿Cuándo vas a hacer tu tarea?	*"When are you going to do your homework?"*
—Voy a leer el libro de texto ahora.	*"I'm going read the textbook now."*

■ **Acabar de** + infinitive means *to have just* done something. It is used to refer to the immediate past:

—¿Quieren Uds. salir a cenar?	*"Do you want to go out for dinner?"*
—No, gracias. Acabamos de cenar.	*"No, thank you. We've just had dinner."*

■ **Tener que** + infinitive means *to have to* do something:

—Tengo que ir de compras. ¿Me acompañas?	*"I have to go shopping. Will you go with me?"*
—Hoy no puedo. Tengo que estar en casa.	*"I can't today. I have to be at home."*

C. **Una receta de cocina** *(A recipe)*. Tell what these people are going to do to prepare dinner. Expand the sentences by adding the **ir a** + infinitive construction.

Modelo   Uds. compran los alimentos. ➤ Uds. van a comprar los alimentos.

1. Concha lee el libro de cocina.

_____

2. Tú encuentras la receta.

_____

3. Nosotros lavamos los vegetales.

_____

4. Mauricio y Florencia prueban el arroz.

_____

5. Ud. añade el aceite de oliva.

_____

6. Yo pongo el pollo al horno.

_____

7. Alicia y Ud. cortan los tomates.

_____

8. Vosotros servís la ensalada.

_____

■ The first-person plural form of **ir, vamos,** can be used with the preposition
a and the infinitive to express *Let's* do something. **Vamos a comer** means
Let's eat, as well as *We're going to eat.* Note that **No vamos a comer** can
only mean *We're not going to eat.*

—**¿Qué hacemos el sábado?**   *"What shall we do on Saturday?"*
—**Vamos a trotar.**   *"Let's go jogging."*

D. El día de mudanza *(Moving day).* You are helping your friends move into
their new house. Answer each person's question about what to do by using
the cue and the **vamos a** + infinitive construction.

Modelo —¿Dónde coloco el televisor? (en el dormitorio)
➤ —Vamos a colocar el televisor en el dormitorio.

En la casa (In the house)

la estantería *bookcase*	**la herramienta** *tool*
la gaveta *drawer*	**los útiles de escuela** *school supplies*

---

1. —¿Dónde pongo los libros? (en la estantería)

— _____

2. —¿Dónde dejo los discos compactos? (al lado del estéreo)

— _____

➤➤➤➤➤

3. —¿Dónde cuelgo este cuadro? (en esa pared)

—_____

4. —¿Dónde guardo las herramientas? (en el garaje)

—_____

5. —¿Dónde meto los útiles de escuela? (en las gavetas del escritorio)

—_____

E. Acabamos de hacerlo todo. When Mrs. Beltrán asks her students when they are going to do certain things, she is surprised to hear that they have already done them. Write the students' responses by using **acabar de** + infinitive.

Modelo   —Gustavo, ¿cuándo vas a cerrar la puerta?
➤ —Acabo de cerrar la puerta, señora.

1. —Pepe, ¿cuándo vas a usar la calculadora?

—_____

2. —Magdalena y Elías, ¿cuándo van a entregar los ensayos?

—_____

3. —¿Cuándo va a borrar la pizarra Ud.?

—_____

4. —Pilar, ¿cuándo vas a tomar el examen?

—_____

5. —¿Cuándo van a hacer los ejercicios Clara y Ester?

—_____

6. —¿Cuándo vais a aprender las fechas de memoria?

—_____

7. —¿Cuándo voy a encontrar mi agenda?

—_____

8. —¿Cuándo vamos a terminar este capítulo?

—_____

F. **¿Cuándo tienen que hacer las actividades?** People have to do certain things at a time different from what their friends think. Write answers to the questions by using the cues and the **tener que** + infinitive construction.

Modelo —¿Sirves los sándwiches más tarde? / ahora
       ➤ —No, tengo que servir los sándwiches ahora.

Frases útiles (Useful phrases)

en punto *on the dot*

lo antes posible *as soon as possible*

---

1. —¿Los ingenieros empiezan el proyecto el miércoles? / hoy

  — _____

2. —¿Ud. devuelve los libros mañana? / esta tarde

  — _____

3. —¿Alquilamos una película ahora mismo? / por la tarde

  — _____

4. —¿El abogado viene a las once? / a las nueve

  — _____

5. —¿Traigo las fotografías la semana próxima? / lo antes posible

  — _____

6. —¿Uds. regresan a Puerto Rico en febrero? / en abril

  — _____

7. —¿Raquel estudia historia este semestre? / el año que viene

  — _____

8. —¿Vosotros oís las noticias a las seis y media? / a las seis en punto

  — _____

Verbs that require a preposition before an infinitive

Some verbs in Spanish require a preposition before an infinitive, but not before a direct object.

- Some verbs that require **a** before an infinitive:

  aprender a *to learn to*
  ayudar a *to help*
  comenzar a (e ➤ ie) *to begin to*
  empezar a (e ➤ ie) *to begin to*
  enseñar a *to show how to; to teach to*

  invitar a *to invite to*
  llegar a *to get to; to succeed in*
  volver a (o ➤ ue) *to do (something) again*

- Some verbs that require **de** before an infinitive:

  dejar de *to stop (doing something)*
  terminar de *to stop*
  tratar de *to try to*

- Some verbs that require **en** before an infinitive:

  insistir en *to insist on*
  quedar en *to agree to*
  tardar en *to delay in; to be long in*

- Some verbs that require **con** before an infinitive:

  contar con (o ➤ ue) *to count on; to rely on*
  soñar con (o ➤ ue) *to dream of/about*

G. *¿A, de, en o con?* Complete each of the following sentences by writing in the missing preposition. Select from **a, de, en,** or **con.**

1. Consuelo y yo quedamos _____ ir al museo el domingo.

2. Los alumnos tratan _____ terminar el informe para el lunes.

3. Yo te ayudo _____ planear la fiesta.

4. Isabel tarda _____ llegar hoy.

5. Luis Alfredo sueña _____ ser millonario.

6. La niña no deja _____ llorar.

7. ¿Llegáis _____ entender la idea?

8. Puedes contar _____ ver a tus amigos allí.

H. Un viaje a Venezuela. Expand each of the following sentences about the Duarte family's trip with the verb in parentheses. Remember that some of the verbs require a preposition before the infinitive.

Modelo   Los Duarte viajan a Venezuela. (querer)
  ➤ Los Duarte quieren viajar a Venezuela.

1. Los Duarte pasan las vacaciones en Caracas. (pensar)

   _____

2. Hacen sus planes para el viaje. (empezar)

   _____

3. Los Duarte visitan a sus parientes en Maracaibo. (quedar)

   _____

4. Mari hace una excursión a La Guaira. (soñar)

   _____

5. Pablo conoce Mérida. (preferir)

   _____

6. La familia Duarte ve lo más posible en cuatro semanas. (tratar)

   _____

En Venezuela

- Venezuela is in the north of South America, on the Caribbean coast. The Spaniards landed in Venezuela in 1498, during Columbus's third voyage to the New World. Alonso de Ojeda happened upon Lake Maracaibo in 1499 and named the new land **Venezuela** or "little Venice" because the Indian pile dwellings reminded him of the Venetian buildings.
- **Caracas,** the capital of Venezuela, has been transformed from a historic colonial town into one of the most modern and impressive cities in Latin America. Founded in 1567, it now has a population of about three million people. It is in the central highlands, about 15 miles from the Caribbean coast where **La Guaira** serves as its port and is the location of popular seaside resorts. **Maracaibo** is Venezuela's second largest city, with a population of around 1,600,000. **Mérida** is the main city in the Andes Mountains region of Venezuela.

I. **Preguntas personales.** Answer the following questions in complete Spanish sentences.

1. ¿Qué quieres hacer este fin de semana?

_____

2. ¿Adónde vas a ir de vacaciones?

_____

3. ¿Qué sueñas con hacer algún día?

_____

4. ¿Qué cosas sabes hacer muy bien?

_____

5. ¿Qué tienes que hacer hoy?

_____

6. ¿Cómo puedes perfeccionar tu español?

_____

7. ¿Qué acabas de hacer?

_____

J. **Composición.** Write a composition of eight to ten sentences about moving day. Mention what you and your friends are going to do, have to do, prefer to do, or intend to do about putting things in order. Use as many verb + infinitive, and verb + preposition (or other word) + infinitive constructions as you can.

Ser and *estar;* Contractions *del* and *al*

I. *Ser* and *estar*

In Spanish, two verbs are equivalent to the English verb *to be:* **ser** and **estar.** Review the conjugations of the present tense of these irregular verbs:

SER *TO BE*		**ESTAR** *TO BE*	
soy	somos	estoy	estamos
eres	sois	estás	estáis
es	son	está	están

The uses of *ser*

■ **Ser** is used to link two nouns or pronouns or a noun and a pronoun. An example is a statement of profession. Note that while English uses the indefinite article *a* or *an* with a profession, Spanish omits the indefinite article **un** or **una.** The indefinite article is used, however, when the profession is modified by an adjective:

Arturo Arce es médico.	*Arturo Arce is a doctor.*
Sandra Rivas es arquitecta.	*Sandra Rivas is an architect.*
Jorge es un ingeniero trabajador.	*Jorge is a hard-working engineer.*

■ **Ser** is followed by phrases that begin with **de** to express origin, possession, and what things are made of:

—**¿De dónde es Ud.?**
—**Soy de España.**
"Where are you from?"
"I'm from Spain."

—**¿De quién es esta calculadora?**
—**Es de Jaime.**
"Whose calculator is this?"
"It's Jaime's."

—**Ese suéter es de lana, ¿no?**

—**No, es de algodón.**
"That sweater is (made of) wool, isn't it?"
"No, it's (made of) cotton."

■ **Ser** is used to express the days of the week, dates, and time, as well as where an event takes place:

—**¿Qué día es hoy?**
—**Hoy es lunes.**
"What day is today?"
"Today is Monday."

—**¿Qué hora es?**
—**Son las tres de la tarde.**
"What time is it?"
"It's 3:00 P.M."

—**¿Dónde es la cena?**

—**Es en el hotel.**
"Where's the dinner?" / "Where does the dinner take place?"
"It's at the hotel."

- **Ser** is used before adjectives that express inherent characteristics and qualities such as nationality, age, physical and moral features, personality, religion, and color:

Mercedes y David son estadounidenses.	*Mercedes and David are American (from the United States).*
Son jóvenes, inteligentes y simpáticos.	*They're young, intelligent, and nice.*
—¿De qué color es tu mochila?	*"What color is your backpack?"*
—Es verde.	*"It's green."*

A. ¿Cuál es su profesión? Write sentences using the verb **ser** and the profession to tell what these people do.

Modelo   Ud. / ingeniero ➤ Ud. es ingeniero.

1. Juliana / fotógrafa

   _____ es _____

2. Clemente y Lorenzo / músicos

   _____ son _____

3. yo / profesora

   _____ soy _____

4. tú / programador de computadoras

   _____ eres _____

5. nosotros / vendedores

   _____ somos _____

6. Isabel y Ud. / dentistas

   _____ son _____

7. Ud. / periodista

   _____ es _____

8. vosotros / hombres de negocios

   _____ sois _____

Note: Some nouns that refer to people end in **-ista** and do not change to distinguish between males and females. However, the article changes to indicate gender: **el/la artista, el/la dentista, el/la periodista, el/la turista.**

B. Nacionalidad y origen. Use forms of **ser** to write sentences that tell the nationality and background of these people.

Modelo   nosotros / Chile / alemán
        ➤ Nosotros somos de Chile. Somos de origen alemán.

1. Magdalena / España / ruso

        es de

2. Uds. / Canadá / japonés

        son de

3. yo / Inglaterra / italiano

        soy de

4. Juan Carlos y Amparo / Costa Rica / irlandés

        son de

5. tú / Francia / árabe

        eres de

6. Paco y yo / los Estados Unidos / español

        somos de

7. Ud. / Colombia / polaco

        es de

8. vosotras / Brasil / portugués

        sois de

C. ¿De qué es? Write sentences with **ser** and the material named to tell what the following items are made of.

Modelo   su blusa / poliéster ➤ Su blusa es de poliéster.

1. el abrigo / lana   *es de*

2. estos juguetes / plástico   *son de*

3. mi vestido / seda   *es de*

4. las camisetas / algodón   *son de*

5. el cinturón / cuero   *es de*

D. ¿De quiénes son estas cosas? Write sentences with **ser** and the person named to show possession.

Modelo el cuaderno / Dorotea ➤ El cuaderno es de Dorotea.

1. esta agenda / Jacobo _____es de_____

2. las llaves / Rosa y Tere _____son de_____

3. esas tijeras / Esteban _____son de_____

4. los bolígrafos / Mari y Álvaro _____son de_____

5. la cartera / Miguel Ángel _____es de_____

E. ¿Cómo son? Tell what these people are like. Write sentences using **ser** and the adjectives that describe their character, personality, or outlook.

Modelo yo *(fem.)* / honesto ➤ Yo soy honesta.

1. tú *(masc.)* / optimista _____eres optimistas_____

2. Rebeca / trabajador _____es_____

3. Guillermo y Virginia / cortés _____son corteses_____

4. yo *(fem.)* / paciente _____soy_____

5. vosotros / realista _____sois realistas_____

F. No son nada parecidos. *(They're not at all alike.)* The people in the following comparisons are nothing alike. Write sentences with **ser** and the adjectives that describe them. (Make sure adjectives and subjects agree.)

Modelo Carlos / simpático : Carlota / antipático
   ➤ Carlos es simpático, pero Carlota es antipática.

1. Juan / pequeño : sus hermanos / grande

   _____es_____ _____son grandes_____

2. los gemelos / egoísta : sus padres / generoso

   _____son egoístas_____ _____son generosos_____

3. tú *(fem.)* / moreno : nosotras / pelirrojo

   _____eres_____ _____somos pelirroja_____

4. Uds. / bajo : su hermana / alto

   son bajos   es alta

5. yo *(fem.)* / cuidadoso : Ud. *(fem.)* / descuidado

   soy cuidadosa   es descuidada

6. Julia / delgado : vosotros / gordo

   es delgada   sois gordos

7. Timoteo / idealista : nosotros / realista

   es   somos realistas

8. mis tíos / agradable : mis primas / molesto

   son agradables   son molestas

The uses of estar

■ **Estar** is used to express permanent or temporary location or position:

La tienda de videos está al lado de la papelería.	*The video store is next to the stationery store.*
Los Espinosa están en París.	*Mr. and Mrs. Espinosa are in Paris.*

■ **Estar** is used to form the progressive tenses: **estar** + the gerund. The gerund is the **-ndo** form of the verb that is the equivalent of the English *-ing* form (see Chapter 5):

—¿**Están estudiando?**	*"Are they studying?"*
—**No, están mirando televisión.**	*"No, they're watching television."*

■ **Estar** is used with adjectives that indicate health, happiness, being busy or tired, or the result of an action, such as a door being opened. The conditions expressed by these adjectives result from a change or express a temporary state:

Estamos bien y contentos.	*We're well and happy.*
La farmacia está abierta.	*The drugstore is open.*

■ Many adjectives that are used with **estar** derive from the past participle of a verb (see Chapter 17). A past participle can be recognized by its ending: **-ado** for **-ar** verbs or **-ido** for **-er** and **-ir** verbs. There are irregular past participles that produce forms such as **abierto** from **abrir** and **roto** *(broken)* from **romper**.

El profesor está ocupado.	*The professor is busy.*
La ventana está rota.	*The window is broken.*

G. **¿Dónde están?** Tell whether these people are on vacation, on a trip, or back home (**de vuelta**). Write sentences with **estar.**

Modelo nosotros / de viaje ➤ Nosotros estamos de viaje.

1. Ignacio / de vacaciones   _está_____

2. Uds. / de vuelta   _están_____

3. yo / en Argentina   _estoy_____

4. mis padres y yo / de viaje   _estamos_____

5. tú / en Italia   _estás_____

6. los Valverde / en Colombia   _está_____

7. Ud. / de vacaciones   _está_____

8. vosotros / en Inglaterra   _estáis_____

H. **En Madrid.** While visiting Madrid, some tourists inquire about where to find certain stores and services. Write sentences with **estar** to tell the location of these places.

Modelo la joyería / al lado de la agencia de viajes
➤ La joyería está al lado de la agencia de viajes.

Tiendas y servicios (Stores and services)	
la peluquería *beauty salon, barber shop*	**la tienda de recuerdos** *souvenir store*
el quiosco *newsstand*	**la tintorería** *dry cleaner*

1. la tintorería / frente al hotel

   _está_____

2. las tiendas de recuerdos / en la Plaza Mayor

   _están_____

3. la peluquería/ en la esquina

   _está_____

4. el correo / en la Plaza de la Cibeles

   _____ *está* _____

5. el quiosco / cerca de la Puerta del Sol

   _____ *está* _____

6. las tiendas de ropa / en la Gran Vía

   _____ *están* _____

7. los restaurantes y cafés / por todas partes

   _____ *están* _____

Lugares de interés en Madrid

- **La Plaza Mayor,** in the heart of old Madrid, was the site of religious ceremonies and royal events. It was built during the reign of Felipe III of the House of Austria in the early seventeenth century. Today, Spaniards and tourists enjoy its outdoor cafés and festivals in summer, the Sunday stamp and coin market, and the typical restaurants and shops that surround the square.
- **La Plaza de la Cibeles,** where **el Paseo del Prado, el Paseo de la Castellana,** and **Alcalá** meet, has a beautiful and famous fountain of the Greek goddess Cybele. Madrid's main post office, **el Palacio de Comunicaciones,** is found here.
- **La Puerta del Sol,** where eight streets and several metro lines intersect, is perhaps the busiest square in Madrid. This square, where people have traditionally met under the clock tower in the police station, is the site of kilometer 0, the point from which all the main roads of Spain are measured.
- **La Gran Vía** is an avenue in downtown Madrid known for its theaters, restaurants, and shops.

I. ¿Cómo están? Tell how these people are feeling. Write sentences with **estar.**

Modelo   Uds. / cansados ➤ Uds. están cansados.

1. tú / feliz

   _____ *estás* _____

2. Marco Antonio y Paloma / desconcertados *(upset)*

   _____ *están* _____

➤➤➤➤➤➤

3. yo / bien

   estoy

4. Leonor / emocionada

   está

5. nosotros / contentos

   estamos

6. Ud. / enfadado

   está

7. Uds. / preocupados

   están

8. vosotros / descansados

   estáis

Adjectives with *ser* and *estar*

■ There are adjectives that can be used with either **ser** or **estar,** but their meaning changes, depending on the choice of the verb. Remember that regardless of the verb used, adjectives must agree with the noun they modify in gender and number:

—¿**Por qué estás aburrida?**	*"Why are you bored?"*
—**Esta novela que leo es aburrida.**	*"This novel I'm reading is boring."*
Estos alumnos son listos.	*These students are smart.*
Todos están listos.	*Everyone is ready.*

■ **Ser** and **estar,** when used with food, convey different meanings:

El helado es delicioso.	*Ice cream is delicious. (general)*
El helado está delicioso.	*The ice cream is (tastes) delicious. (specific)*

J. *¿Ser o estar?* Complete each of the following sentences by writing the correct form of either **ser** or **estar**.

1. Francisco siempre ___es___ gracioso.

2. ¿Tú ___estás___ de acuerdo?

3. Estos anillos ___son___ de oro.   *gold ring*

4. ¿De dónde ___eres___ tú?

5. Yo ___estoy___ muy contenta hoy.

6. Nosotros ___estamos___ de viaje todavía.

7. Yo ___soy___ de origen inglés.

8. Acabo de probar la sopa. ___está___ muy sabrosa.   *finish trying soup*

9. Diego y yo ___somos___ estudiantes.

10. ¿Uds. ya ___están___ listos para salir?   *ready*

11. Nola ___está___ pálida porque ___está___ acatarrada.   *pale   cold*

12. Yo no ___estoy___ de acuerdo con Uds.

K. El álbum de fotos. Rosaura is showing her photo album to a friend. She describes the members of her family as they appear in the photos. Write the correct form of either **ser** or **estar** to complete the sentences.

Este libro ___es___ (1) mi álbum de fotos. Mira la foto que

___está___ (2) a la derecha. Yo ___soy___ (3) con mis papás y mis

hermanos. En esa foto que _____ (4) abajo puedes ver a mi hermana

Regina. Ella ___es___ (5) actriz. El hombre que _____ (6)

a su lado _____ (7) su esposo. Mi cuñado Roberto _____ (8)

ingeniero. ¿Y ves a los dos niños que _____ (9) sentados en el sofá?

_____ (10) mis sobrinos Miguelito y Aurorita. Aunque no lo parecen,

_____ (11) muy traviesos.

II. The Contractions *del* and *al*

- The masculine definite article **el** combines with the preposition **de** to form **del** and with the preposition **a** to form **al**. **De** and **a** do not contract with the other forms of the definite article **la**, **los**, and **las**:

La biblioteca del colegio tiene pocos libros.	*The school library has few books.*
La librería de la universidad es excelente.	*The university bookstore is excellent.*
¿Vuelves al estadio ahora?	*Are you going back to the stadium now?*

- The contractions are not used if the definite article is part of a proper name:

—Vamos a El Salvador este verano.	*"We're going to El Salvador this summer."*
—¡Qué casualidad! Yo soy de El Salvador.	*"What a coincidence! I'm from El Salvador."*

L. **¿*A o de*?** Complete each of the following sentences by adding **a** or **de**. Write contractions as necessary and cross out the extra definite article.

1. El consultorio es _____ el médico.

2. Elena va _____ el centro comercial esta tarde.

3. La computadora es _____ la programadora.

4. Vamos _____ El Prado el sábado.

5. El tren _____ las ocho llega tarde.

6. Tienen que ver _____ el profesor Maldonado.

7. Las herramientas son _____ el mecánico.

8. ¿Cuándo vas a ir _____ el banco?

M. Preguntas personales. Answer the following questions in complete Spanish sentences.

1. ¿De qué origen eres?

   _____

2. ¿Dónde está tu casa o apartamento?

   _____

3. ¿Cuál es la profesión de tu padre? (tu madre / tus hermanos)

   _____

4. ¿Cómo es tu mejor amigo o amiga?

   _____

5. ¿Cómo estás hoy?

   _____

6. ¿De qué colores es la ropa que llevas hoy?

   _____

7. ¿De dónde son los estudiantes extranjeros del colegio?

   _____

8. Cuando vas de vacaciones, ¿adónde prefieres ir?

   _____

N. Composición. Write a composition of eight to ten sentences in which you describe yourself. Tell what you look like and what some of your character and personality traits are.

The Present Progressive

- The present progressive tense is made up of the present tense of the verb **estar** (see Chapter 4) followed by the present participle or gerund (**-ndo** form). The present participle in Spanish is equivalent to the *-ing* form in English (for example, *listening*). For **-ar** verbs, the ending of the present participle is **-ando;** for **-er** and **-ir** verbs, the ending is **-iendo:**

  visitar ➤ **visitando**   comer ➤ **comiendo**   abrir ➤ **abriendo**

- When **-ir** verbs have a stem change in the present tense, the vowel of the stem also changes in the present participle:

  decir ➤ **diciendo**   sentir ➤ **sintiendo**

  dormir ➤ **durmiendo**   servir ➤ **sirviendo**

  morir ➤ **muriendo**   venir ➤ **viniendo**

  pedir ➤ **pidiendo**

- For -er and **-ir** verbs whose stem ends in a vowel, **-iendo** changes to **-yendo** in the present participle:

  leer ➤ **leyendo**   construir ➤ **construyendo**

  traer ➤ **trayendo**   oír ➤ **oyendo**

- The verbs **poder** and **ir** have irregular gerunds:

  poder ➤ **pudiendo**   ir ➤ **yendo**

- The present progressive tense is used to refer to actions that are happening right now or that have just begun. In Spanish, the present progressive can never refer to the future as the English present progressive can. To refer to the future in Spanish, we use the simple present tense or the **ir a** + infinitive construction: *We're arriving on Wednesday* = **Llegamos el miércoles** or **Vamos a llegar el miércoles.**

  —Carlos está haciendo su tarea, ¿no?

  —¡Qué va! Está trotando en el parque.

  "Carlos is doing his homework, isn't he?"

  "Are you kidding? He's jogging in the park."

- In the present progressive construction, direct or indirect object pronouns are either placed before the verb **estar** or attached to the present participle. (See Chapter 11 to review direct and indirect object pronouns.) In writing, an accent mark is added over the **a** or **e** of the participle ending when one or more object pronouns are attached:

—Uds. tienen que escribir las cartas pronto. *"You have to write the letters soon."*

—Estamos escribiéndolas ahora mismo.

—Las estamos escribiendo ahora. *"We're writing them right now."*

A. El gerundio. Write the gerund (present participle) for each of the following verbs.

1. ayudar _____

2. ocurrir _____

3. encontrar _____

4. creer _____

5. seguir _____

6. enviar _____

7. construir _____

8. platicar _____

9. sentir _____

10. leer _____

B. ¡Están disfrutando! Tell how these people are celebrating Paquito's birthday. Use the cues to write sentences in the present progressive.

Modelo Paquito / celebrar su cumpleaños
➤ Paquito está celebrando su cumpleaños.

Palabras para una fiesta (Words for a party)

el globo *balloon*

hacer reventar *to burst*

jugar al escondite *to play hide-and-seek*

---

1. su mamá / servir la torta

_____

2. su papá y su tío / tomar fotos

_____

3. Carmencita y yo / romper la piñata

_____

➤➤➤➤➤

4. tú / abrir los regalos

_____

5. Uds. / jugar al escondite

_____

6. yo / traer el helado

_____

7. Juanito / hacer reventar los globos

_____

8. vosotros / oír la música

_____

C. Son las siete de la mañana. Write sentences in the present progressive to tell what these people are doing at seven o'clock in the morning.

Modelo   Uds. / preparar el café
        ➤ Uds. están preparando el café.

1. yo / dormir como un tronco *(to sleep soundly/like a log)*

_____

2. Ud. / leer el periódico

_____

3. los señores Martínez / coger el tren

_____

4. tú / poner la mesa

_____

5. Carolina / meter los libros en la mochila

_____

6. nosotros / ver las noticias en la tele

_____

7. Uds. / comer pan tostado

_____

8. vosotros / correr por el parque

_____

D. Los días de fiesta. Tell what people are doing during the holiday celebrations. Write sentences in the present progressive.

Modelo   Ud. / tomar fotos ➤ Ud. está tomando fotos.

Más palabras para una fiesta

envolver (o ➤ ue) _to wrap (gifts, packages)_
el villancico _Christmas carol_

---

1. la abuela / preparar yemas de Santa Teresa

_____

2. Paloma y yo / envolver los regalos

_____

3. Uds. / escribir tarjetas de Navidad

_____

4. el coro / cantar villancicos

_____

5. tú / servir refrescos y galletas

_____

6. yo / decorar la sala

_____

7. Gregorio / arreglar las velas

_____

8. vosotros / escoger los discos compactos

_____

La Navidad

- **Las yemas de Santa Teresa** (Santa Teresa egg-yolk candy) are served in Spain around the Christmas season. This candy is named for Santa Teresa de Jesús, the Spanish mystic who was born and died in Ávila (1515–1582). She was a prolific and influential writer, as well as a religious reformer.
- The Spanish **villancico** is a popular song with a religious theme that is sung at Christmas time. Christmas is a time for families to get together and for friends to give each other **cestas de Navidad** (Christmas baskets). These wicker baskets are filled with foodstuffs such as **turrón** (hard candy made of almonds, sugar, honey, and egg whites), **mazapán** (marzipan, candy made of almond paste and sugar), **almendras garrapiñadas** (sugar-coated almonds), ham, and refreshments. Traditionally, the time for giving gifts is **el Día de los Reyes,** or **Epifanía** (Epiphany), which is celebrated on January 6. The **roscón de Reyes** (Twelfth-Night cake) is customarily eaten on this day. The cake is baked with a lima bean or a small glass animal figurine inside. It is believed that the person who gets the lima bean or the figurine in his or her piece of cake will have good luck for the whole year.

E. En el salón de clase. Tell what people are doing in class. Write sentences in the present progressive. For each item, write one sentence attaching the object pronoun to the present participle. (Do not forget to add the accent mark.) Then, write another sentence placing the object pronoun before **estar.**

Modelo   Leo / hacer preguntas
➤ Leo está haciéndolas. / Leo las está haciendo.

1. los alumnos / tomar los exámenes

_____

_____

2. el profesor Alberti / dictar una conferencia *(to give a lecture)*

_____

_____

3. tú / repasar la lección

_____

_____

4. Mercedes y Ud. / leer un poema en voz alta

_____

_____

5. yo / resolver problemas de álgebra

_____

_____

6. Manolo / colgar un mapa de Sudamérica

_____

_____

7. Vera y yo / borrar la pizarra

_____

_____

8. vosotras / pedir ayuda

_____

_____

F. **¡Ahora!** Write questions asking when people will do certain things. Then write answers to the questions saying that people are doing these things now. Change direct object nouns to pronouns in your responses. Write dashes for dialogue exchanges.

Modelo Federico / escribir el informe
   ➤ —¿Cuándo va Federico a escribir el informe?
      —Está escribiéndolo ahora.

1. Uds. / fotocopiar los artículos

_____

_____

2. Anita / usar la calculadora

_____

_____

➤➤➤➤➤

3. tú / recibir el mensaje

_____

_____

4. Teo y Rafa / reparar la impresora (*printer*)

_____

_____

5. Ud. / llamar al dentista

_____

_____

6. los primos / devolver los libros

_____

_____

G. ¿Cómo pasas el día? Tell how people spend their day. Change the cue verb to the gerund form in your answer.

Modelo   Nora / hablar por teléfono
➤ Nora pasa el día hablando por teléfono.

Palabras útiles

el césped *lawn*   **navegar en el web** *to surf on the web*
los dibujos animados *cartoons*

---

1. David y yo / jugar al tenis

_____

2. Mauricio / navegar en el web

_____

3. tú / ver dibujos animados

_____

4. Uds. / escribir su informe

   _____

5. Laura y Ernesto / andar en bicicleta

   _____

6. yo / organizar mi escritorio

   _____

7. Silvia / leer revistas de modas

   _____

8. vosotros / cortar el césped

   _____

H. **Preguntas personales.** Answer the following questions in complete Spanish sentences.

1. ¿Qué estás estudiando este año?

   _____

2. ¿De qué están hablando tus compañeros de clase?

   _____

3. ¿Qué está diciendo el profesor/la profesora?

   _____

4. ¿En qué estás pensando?

   _____

5. ¿Qué libros estás leyendo últimamente *(lately)*?

   _____

I. **Composición.** Write a composition of eight to ten sentences in which you tell what you and other people are doing now that you and they were not doing before. Use the present progressive to describe these activities.

CHAPTER

6

Nouns; Definite Articles; The Neuter Article *lo*; Indefinite Articles

I. Nouns

Gender

- All Spanish nouns are either masculine or feminine; that is, they all have gender. Most nouns that end in -**o** or that refer to males are masculine:

el concierto	**el padre**	**el programador**

- Most nouns that end in -**a** or that refer to females are feminine:

la biblioteca	**la madre**	**la programadora**

- Many Spanish nouns that end in -**a** and -**ma** are masculine. Likewise, some nouns that end in -**o** are feminine:

masculine	feminine
el mapa	**la foto** (from **la fotografía**)
el día	**la mano**
el idioma	**la radio**
el programa	

- Because the gender of nouns that end in -**e** or a consonant cannot be predicted, it is necessary to memorize whether they are masculine or feminine:

masculine	feminine
el cine	**la gente**
el deporte	**la llave**
el papel	**la calle**
el examen	**la legumbre**
el reloj	**la nariz**

- The days of the week, the months of the year, and the names of languages are masculine:

Vamos a llamarte el viernes o el sábado.	*We're going to call you on Friday or Saturday.*
Éste es el abril más lluvioso.	*This is the rainiest April.*
El español y el francés son lenguas romances, es decir, vienen del latín.	*Spanish and French are Romance languages, that is, they come from Latin.*

- Nouns that end in **-dad, -tad, -tud, -ión, -umbre, -cia, -ie, -ez, -sis,** and **-itis** are usually feminine:

la ciudad	**la diferencia**
la dificultad	**la serie** *(series)*
la juventud *(youth)*	**la sencillez** *(simplicity)*
la información	**la dosis**
la muchedumbre *(crowd)*	**la poliomielitis** *(polio)*

- Nouns that end in **-aje, -or, -án, -ambre,** or a stressed vowel are usually masculine:

el paisaje	**el alambre** *(wire)*
el calor	**el sofá**
el refrán *(proverb)*	**el champú**

- Spanish nouns that refer to people (and some animals) that end in **-or, -és, -ón,** and **-ín** are usually masculine. These nouns add **-a** to form the feminine:

masculine	feminine
el profesor	**la profesora**
el inglés	**la inglesa**
el ladrón *(thief)*	**la ladrona**
el bailarín *(dancer)*	**la bailarina**

- Nouns that refer to people and that end in **-e, -a, -ista,** or **-nte** do not change for the feminine form. Instead, the article indicates whether the noun refers to a male or a female:

el / la intérprete *(interpreter)*	**el / la dentista**
el / la atleta	**el / la estudiante**

   Note: Often, in everyday speech, nouns ending in **-nte** are given a feminine form ending in **-nta: la estudianta, la clienta.** Another exception is the noun **la jefa** *(female boss)*.

- Compound nouns in Spanish that consist of a verb and a noun are masculine:

el sacapuntas	**el lavaplatos**	**el tocadiscos**

- Feminine nouns that begin with a stressed **a-** or **ha-** take the masculine article **el** in the singular to avoid a double "ah" sound. Even though they take the article **el,** these nouns are feminine. They take the feminine article **las** in the plural:

el agua fría	**las aguas frías**
el hambre	
el alma *(soul, spirit)*	**las almas**

A. ¿Masculino o femenino? Write the masculine or feminine form of the definite article next to each noun.

1. ___la___ computadora
2. ___el___ sello
3. ___el___ pie
4. ___el___ televisor

5. ___el___ idioma
6. ___la___ belleza
7. ___el___ alma
8. ___el___ paraguas

B. La política. Write the masculine or feminine form of the definite article next to each noun. Each noun has to do with some aspect of politics.

1. ___el___ gobierno
2. ___la___ unión
3. ___la___ comunidad
4. ___el___ comité
5. ___la___ jefe de estado

6. ___la___ economía
7. ___el___ presidente
8. ___la___ moneda
9. ___el___ sistema
10. ___el___ congreso

La Unión Europea

Spain is a member of **la Unión Europea** (European Union), which began as **la Comunidad Económica Europea** (European Economic Community) in 1958 before becoming known as **la Comunidad Europea** (European Community) until 1994. The goal of the European Union is to integrate the democratic nations of Europe politically, economically, and socially. At present there is a free flow of goods, services, capital, and persons within the **Unión Europea.** Eleven countries, including Spain, have signed on to form **la Unión Económica y Monetaria** (Economic and Monetary Union), which was set to begin in January 1999. The member countries will adopt a common currency (**la moneda única**) called the *euro*. The fifteen countries that make up the European Union are Austria, Belgium, Denmark, Finland, France, Germany, Greece, Ireland, Italy, Luxembourg, the Netherlands, Portugal, Spain, Sweden, and the United Kingdom.

C. Las profesiones. Write the missing noun that is the masculine or feminine professional counterpart in each pair of nouns.

1. _el banquer_   la banquera

2. el periodista   _la periodista_

3. el director de cine   _la directora_

4. _el ingeniero_   la ingeniera

5. el escultor   *la escultora*

6. *el fotógrafo*   la fotógrafa

7. el contable   *la contable*

8. *el escritor*   la escritora

D. Para el almuerzo. Tell what foods are on the table for lunch by writing in the correct form of the definite article for each item.

1. *el* jamón   7. *el* pastel

2. *el* arroz   8. *la* ensalada

3. *la* salsa picante   9. *el* leche

4. *el* flan   10. *el* salmón

5. *el* carne   11. *el* azúcar

6. *el* café   12. *la* tarta de manzana

Number

■ In Spanish, nouns that end in a vowel form the plural by adding -s:

singular	plural
el piano	**los pianos**
la obra	**las obras**
el guante	**los guantes**

■ Nouns that end in a consonant form the plural by adding -es:

singular	plural
el examen	**los exámenes**
el joven	**los jóvenes**
el país	**los países**
el lápiz	**los lápices**
la pared	**las paredes**
la reunión	**las reuniones**

Notes:

1. Nouns that are stressed on the last syllable in the singular lose their accent mark in the plural: **reunión ➤ reuniones.** An exception is **país ➤ países.**

2. Nouns that have a written accent mark on the next-to-last syllable in the singular keep the accent mark in the plural: **lápiz ➤ lápices.** Note that **z** changes to **c** before the plural ending **-es.**

3. **Examen** and **joven** add an accent mark in the plural: **examen ➤ exámenes, joven ➤ jóvenes.**

■ Nouns of more than one syllable ending in an unstressed vowel plus **s** do not add a plural ending:

el viernes	**los viernes**
el paraguas	**los paraguas**

■ The masculine plural of nouns that refer to people includes both males and females, as well as males only:

los hijos	*children; sons and daughters; sons*

■ Some nouns are always used in the plural in Spanish:

los gemelos	*twins; binoculars; cufflinks*
los anteojos	*eyeglasses*
las gafas	*eyeglasses*
las tijeras	*scissors*
las vacaciones	*vacation*
las afueras	*outskirts*

Notes:

1. Foreign words (usually English) that have been incorporated into Spanish are almost always masculine: **el film, el golf, el hockey, el jazz, el marketing, el récord.**

2. If a proper name refers to a family, it has no plural form: **los Zamora** *(the Zamora family)*, **los Sánchez** *(the Sánchezes).*

E. En plural. Write the plural form of these nouns and their articles.

1. el teatro _____

2. la cartera _____

3. la estación _____

4. el irlandés _____

5. el viernes _____

6. el lápiz _____

7. el sacapuntas _____

8. la edad _____

9. el mes _____

10. la reunión _____

11. el español _____

12. el joven _____

13. la luz _____

14. el cajón _____

15. el collar _____

II. Definite Articles

■ In Spanish, the definite article (*the* in English) changes its form to agree with the noun in gender (masculine or feminine) and number (singular or plural):

	masculine	feminine
singular	el	la
plural	los	las
	el museo	la ciencia
	los museos	las ciencias

■ In Spanish, unlike in English, the definite article is used before a noun to talk about something in a general way. When used as nouns, colors require the definite article:

Gozamos de la libertad individual en los Estados Unidos.	*We have (enjoy) individual freedom in the United States.*
El chocolate es delicioso.	*Chocolate is delicious.*
El rojo es mi color favorito.	*Red is my favorite color.*

■ The definite article **el** is used before the names of languages. It is not used directly after **hablar** and the prepositions **de** and **en**. It is usually omitted after the verbs **aprender, enseñar, estudiar, leer, practicar,** and **saber:**

Rosa habla italiano, ¿no?	*Rosa speaks Italian, doesn't she?*
El profesor Robles enseña sus clases de historia en español.	*Professor Robles teaches his history classes in Spanish.*
No encuentro los libros de ruso.	*I can't find the Russian books.*

■ The definite article is used before titles, except when the person is addressed directly:

—**Señor Iriarte, ¿está Ud. de acuerdo con nosotros?**	*"Mr. Iriarte, do you agree with us?"*
—**Yo sí, pero el señor Sánchez no está de acuerdo.**	*"I agree, but Mr. Sánchez doesn't agree."*

- The definite article is used with the days of the week, except after **ser**:

  —¿Vas al teatro el miércoles?   *"Are you going to the theater on Wednesday?"*

  —No, siempre voy los viernes.   *"No, I always go on Fridays."*

  Hoy es lunes.   *Today is Monday.*

- The definite article is often, but not always, used with the names of the seasons:

  —Voy a hacer un viaje en la primavera.   *"I'm going to take a trip in the spring."*

  —Yo prefiero viajar en invierno.   *"I prefer to travel in winter."*

- The definite article is used to express the time of day:

  —Pensamos volver a las ocho.   *"We intend to be back at eight o'clock."*

  —¡Pero ya son las seis y media!   *"But it's already 6:30!"*

- The definite article is used in Spanish with parts of the body and articles of clothing, whereas in English the possessive adjective is normally used:

  Tengo el pie izquierdo más grande que el pie derecho.   *My left foot is bigger than my right foot.*

  ¿Te duele el estómago?   *Does your stomach hurt?*

  Los niños se ponen los guantes.   *The children are putting on their gloves.*

- The definite article is traditionally used before the names of some countries. However, current usage tends to omit it. The definite article must be used before the name of a country, city, or continent that is modified:

  —Yo soy de (los) Estados Unidos. ¿Y Uds.?   *"I'm from the United States. And what about you?"*

  —Yo soy de(l) Canadá.   *"I'm from Canada."*

  —Y yo soy de África. Del África oriental.   *"And I'm from Africa. From East Africa."*

- The definite article is omitted before mass or count nouns that refer to an unspecified quantity or to some or part of the whole of their class:

  Felisa está tomando vitaminas.   *Felisa is taking vitamins. (some vitamins)*

  Compran pan.   *They buy bread. (some bread)*

  Hay bombones en la caja.   *There are candies in the box.*

- Multiple-word compound nouns in Spanish consist of noun + **de** + noun, with no definite article before the second noun:

  el libro de química   *the chemistry book*

  la clase de historia   *the history class*

F. Artículo definido + sustantivo. Complete the following chart by filling in the blank spaces with the correct form of the singular definite article and writing out the plural definite article and noun.

singular definite article + noun	plural definite article + noun
1. _el_ grupo	_los grupos_
2. _la_ chaqueta	_las chaquetas_
3. _el_ gol	_los goles_
4. _la_ llave	_las llaves_
5. _el_ desfile	_los desfiles_
6. _la_ mano	_las manos_
7. _el_ jueves	_los jueves_
8. _la_ nacionalidad	_las nacionalidades_
9. _el_ avión	_los aviónes_
10. _la_ serie	_las series_
11. _el_ ascensor	_los ascensores_
12. _el_ francés	_los francés_
13. _la_ nariz	_las narices_
14. _el_ lavaplatos	_los lavaplatos_
15. _la_ pez	_las peces_

G. La Madre Naturaleza (Mother Nature). Beti and her family love being close to nature. Tell about their interests by filling in the blank spaces with the correct form of the definite article.

1. A Beti le encanta _la_ naturaleza.

2. Beti, sus padres y hermanos salen de la ciudad para ver _el_ paisaje.

3. A veces van a un parque en _el_ campo o a una casita en _la_ sierra.

4. A Javier le gustan _los_ animales, especialmente _los_ pájaros.

5. A Margarita le fascinan _los_ árboles y _las_ flores.

6. Esta vez la familia va a _la_ costa para ver _el_ mar.

⋙⋙⋙

7. __el__ bebé Hernandito está contento jugando en __la__ arena.

8. Por la noche, todos caminan en __la__ playa viendo __las__ estrellas y escuchando __las__ olas.

H. ¿Con el artículo definido o no? Fill in the blanks with the correct form of the definite article where it is needed. Mark the space with an *X* if the definite article is not required.

1. __la__ profesora Dalí está haciendo investigaciones *(doing research)* en __la__ biblioteca.

2. Mañana es __X__ martes.

3. __el__ azúcar no es bueno para __la__ salud.

4. No hay __las__ toallas en __el__ armario.

5. __el__ señor Núñez, ¿lee Ud. en __el__ alemán?

6. Aunque prefiero __el__ otoño, me gusta __el__ invierno también.

7. Piensan regresar a casa para __X__ cuatro y media de la tarde.

8. Elías no encuentra el libro de __X__ química.

III. The Neuter Article *lo*

■ Spanish has a neuter article **lo** that is used before a masculine adjective to mean *that which is*. Notice the different ways to express **lo** + adjective in English:

lo bueno	*the good part, what's good*
lo fácil	*the easy thing, the easy aspect*
Hay que buscar lo hermoso de la vida.	*One should seek the beautiful things (what's beautiful) in life.*

■ **Lo,** used in the phrase **lo que,** means *what,* but not as an interrogative:

Yo no comprendo lo que dices.	*I don't understand what you're saying.*
Lo que nos interesa es la música.	*What interests us is music.*

I. *Lo* **+ adjetivo.** Express the following phrases in Spanish using the
lo + adjective construction to complete the sentences.

1. _____ *(The interesting part)* del libro es el último
capítulo.

2. _____ *(The important thing)* es tener el correo
electrónico.

3. Gerardo siempre trata de hacer _____ *(the
impossible).*

4. Los rascacielos son _____ *(the modern part)* de la
ciudad.

5. _____ *(The best part)* de la comida es el postre.

6. Pensamos menos en _____ *(old stuff)* para el año
nuevo.

7. _____ *(What's strange)* es que Emilia no encuentra
su licencia de manejar.

8. _____ *(The boring thing)* de la obra de teatro es
el principio.

J. *¿Lo que o que?* Complete each of the following sentences by writing either
lo que or **que.**

1. Puedes comer _____ quieres.

2. ¿No saben _____ Pedro llega mañana?

3. Marcos y Mari siempre creen _____ leen.

4. Nos parece _____ la librería Sol está en esta calle.

5. No encuentro _____ busco.

6. Dicen _____ va a nevar esta tarde.

7. No comprendemos _____ hace Carmen.

8. _____ les gusta más es patinar sobre el hielo.

IV. Indefinite Articles

- In Spanish, the indefinite article (*a* and *an* in English) changes its form to agree with the noun. It is masculine or feminine and singular or plural:

	masculine	feminine
singular	un	una
plural	unos	unas

- The plural indefinite articles **unos** and **unas** are equivalent to *some, a few,* and *a couple* in English:

Discuten unos temas.	*They're arguing about some topics.*
¿Me prestas unos lápices?	*Can you lend me a few pencils?*

- **Un,** instead of **una,** is used with feminine nouns that begin with a stressed a- or ha-:

el / un agua	**las / unas aguas**
el / un área	**las / unas áreas**

- Used with the verb **ser,** the indefinite article is omitted before nouns of profession, occupation, nationality, and religion. If the noun is modified, however, the indefinite article must be used:

Manuel es cocinero.	*Manuel is a chef.*
Es un cocinero excelente.	*He's an excellent chef.*

- The indefinite article is usually omitted after the verbs **tener, comprar, buscar, llevar** *(to wear)*, **usar,** and **sacar:**

Roberto tiene perro.	*Roberto has a dog.*
Lleva corbata todos los días.	*He wears a tie every day.*

- The indefinite article is omitted in phrases with **¡qué...!** *(what a ...!)* and before **otro, cierto, tal, medio, ciento,** and **mil.** Note that the equivalent phrases in English use the indefinite article:

¡Qué idea!	*What an idea!*
Hacemos otro viaje en marzo.	*We're taking another trip in March.*
¡No voy a decir tal cosa nunca!	*I'll never say such a thing!*

K. Artículo indefinido + sustantivo. Complete the following chart by filling in the blank spaces with the correct form of the singular indefinite article and writing out the plural indefinite article and noun.

singular indefinite article + noun	plural indefinite article + noun
1. _una_ finca	_unas fincas_
2. _un_ sándwich	_unos sandwiches_
3. _un_ limón	_unos limónes_
4. _una_ japonés	_unos japoneses_
5. _el_ nube	_____
6. _un_ área	_unas áreas_
7. _una_ ciudad	_unas ciudades_
8. _una_ voz	_las voces_
9. _una_ limpiaparabrisas	_unas limpiaparabrisas_
10. _un_ dirección	_unos direccónes_
11. _un_ agua	_unas aguas_
12. _una_ esperanza	_unas esperanzas_
13. _un_ problema	_unos problemas_
14. _una_ libertad	_unas libertades_
15. _un_ sabor	_unos sabores_

L. En el almacén. Tell what items of clothing people are shopping for in the department store. Write the correct form of the indefinite article.

1. Teodoro busca _una_ corbata gris.

2. Uds. necesitan _unos_ zapatos de tenis.

3. ¿No encuentras _un_ suéter de lana?

4. Acabamos de ver _unos_ guantes muy bonitos.

5. Ud. quiere _una_ blusa de manga (*sleeve*) larga.

6. Paco y Rafa necesitan _unas_ camisetas de algodón.

7. Yo debo comprar _uno_ abrigo nuevo.

8. Queréis _unos_ jeans azules, ¿verdad?

M. ¿Con el artículo indefinido o no? Fill in the blanks with the correct form of the indefinite article where it is needed. Mark the space with an *X* if the indefinite article is not required.

1. Estamos pasando ___un___ día muy agradable.

2. ¡Qué ___X___ situación más complicada!

3. Isabel Mondragón es ___una___ pintora muy conocida.

4. Tienes que comprar ___X___ medio kilo de uvas y ___un___ kilo de manzanas.

5. Les voy a prestar ___X___ mil dólares.

6. Hay ___unas___ turistas chilenos y colombianos en el hotel.

7. Están leyendo ___unas___ revistas francesas.

8. ¡No comprendemos tal ___una___ cosa!

N. Preguntas personales. Answer the following questions in complete Spanish sentences.

1. ¿Cuál es la profesión de tu papá/tu mamá?

_____

2. ¿Qué es lo que te interesa más?

_____

3. ¿Cuáles son tus colores favoritos?

_____

4. ¿Qué ropa necesitas comprar?

_____

5. ¿Qué alimentos son buenos o malos para la salud?

_____

O. Composición. Write a composition of eight to ten sentences describing the items you find in your closet (**el armario**) or in a dresser drawer (**una gaveta del tocador**). Focus on nouns and on using or omitting the definite and indefinite articles as you talk about the nouns.

Personal *a*; Negative and Indefinite Words; Saber and conocer; Question Formation

I. The Personal *a*

■ In Spanish, a direct object noun follows its verb directly, without a preposition, if it refers to a thing:

—Tere, ¿buscas tu cartera todavía?	*"Tere, are you still looking for your wallet?"*
—Claro que no. ¡Ahora, busco mis llaves!	*"Of course not. Now I'm looking for my keys!"*

■ A direct object noun that refers to a specific person is preceded by the personal **a**:

—David, ¿buscas *a* la programadora?	*"David, are you looking for the programmer?"*
—Sí, y busco *al* gerente también.	*"Yes, and I'm looking for the manager too."*

Note: In the above examples, the nouns **cartera, llaves, programadora,** and **gerente** are direct objects.

■ The personal **a** is used before indefinite pronouns, such as **alguien** *(someone)*, **nadie** *(nobody)*, and **alguno** and **ninguno** when they refer to people. The personal **a** is used in the question phrases **¿a quién?** and **¿a quiénes?** *(to whom?):*

—¿Esperas a alguien?	*"Are you waiting for someone?"*
—No, no espero a nadie.	*"No, I'm not waiting for anyone."*
—Yo voy a ver a algunos amigos hoy.	*"I'm going to see some friends today."*
—¿A quién llevas al concierto?	*"Whom are you taking to the concert?"*
—Llevo a Irene.	*"I'm taking Irene."*

■ The personal **a** is not used before nouns that refer to people as a general group:

—Nuestra empresa necesita arquitectos.	*"Our company needs architects."* (general)
—También buscamos un contable bilingüe.	*"We're also looking for a bilingual accountant."*

Note: The personal **a** is usually not used with **tener: Tengo dos hermanos y una hermana.**

- Some verbs that take a direct object in Spanish (whose English equivalents have a preposition):

  buscar algo / a alguien *to look for something / someone (specific)*

  cuidar a alguien *to take care of someone*

  escuchar algo / a alguien *to listen to something / someone*

  esperar algo / a alguien *to wait for something / someone*

  mirar algo / a alguien *to look at something / someone*

A. La *a* personal. Complete the following sentences by writing in the personal **a** (or the contraction **al**) where it is necessary. Write an *X* in the space if the personal **a** is not needed.

> ### Vocabulario útil (Useful vocabulary)
>
> **el botiquín** *first-aid kit; medicine cabinet*
> **la niñera** *babysitter*

1. Estoy escuchando ___X___ el nuevo disco compacto.

2. Marisol no comprende ___a___ la profesora.

3. Ayudamos ___a___ la niñera a cuidar ___al___ el niño.

4. La compañía necesita ___X___ secretarios bilingües.

5. ¿Por qué no buscas ___X___ la medicina en el botiquín?

6. No vamos a invitar ___a___ Alberto a la fiesta.

7. ¿Cuándo lleváis ___al___ el coche ___al___ el mecánico?

8. Espero ver _____ los Maldonado en Madrid.

B. ¿Cuál es la traducción? *(Which one is the translation?)* Circle the letter of the Spanish sentence that correctly expresses the English one. Focus on the use of the personal **a.**

1. I'm looking for a bilingual secretary.
   a. Busco a la secretaria bilingüe.
   b. Busco una secretaria bilingüe.

2. Whom are they inviting?
   a. ¿A quiénes invitan?
   b. ¿Quiénes invitan?

3. They plan to see some of these people.
   a. Piensan ver a algunos.
   b. Piensan ver algunos.

4. She doesn't understand the lawyer.
   a. No comprende el abogado.
   b. No comprende al abogado.

5. You're looking at someone.

    a. Mira a alguien.   b. Mira alguien.

6. Nobody takes care of the children.

    a. Los niños no cuidan a nadie.   b. Nadie cuida a los niños.

II. Negative and Indefinite Words

■ Study the following list of Spanish negative words and expressions and their affirmative counterparts:

Negative Words and Expressions	Affirmative Counterparts
nada *nothing*	**algo** *something*
nadie *no one, nobody*	**alguien** *someone, somebody*
nunca / jamás *never*	**alguna vez** *sometime* **algunas veces** *sometimes* **a veces** *sometimes* **muchas veces / a menudo** *often* **siempre** *always*
nunca más *never again*	**otra vez** *again*
ni / ni siquiera *not even*	**o** *or*
ni... ni... *neither . . . nor*	**o... o...** *either . . . or*
ninguno (ningún), ninguna *no, not a*	**alguno (algún), alguna** *some*
tampoco *neither, not either*	**también** *also, too*
en / por ninguna parte *nowhere*	**en / por alguna parte** *somewhere*
en / por ningún lado / sitio / lugar *nowhere*	**en / por algún lado / sitio / lugar** *somewhere*
de ninguna manera *in no way*	**de alguna manera** *in some way, somehow*
de ningún modo *in no way*	**de algún modo** *in some way, somehow*
ya no *no longer*	**todavía** *still*

Notes:

1. **Alguno** and **ninguno** are shortened to **algún** and **ningún,** respectively, before a masculine singular noun:

    —Creo que Diana trabaja en   *"I think Diana works in some*
      algún almacén por aquí.   *department store around here."*
    —Pero no hay ningún almacén   *"But there's no department store*
      cerca.   *nearby."*

2. **Ninguno** is followed by a singular noun unless the noun is always used in the plural:

    No encuentro ningunas tijeras.   *I can't find any scissors.*

- When a negative word follows the verb, the word **no** precedes it in the sentence:

  —**Juan y yo** *no* **vamos** *nunca* **a ese café.**   *"Juan and I never go to that café."*

  —**Yo** *no* **voy** *tampoco.*   *"I don't go (there) either."*

- When a negative word precedes the verb, then **no** is not used:

  —**Juan y yo** *nunca* **vamos a ese café.**   *"Juan and I never go to that café."*

  —**Yo** *tampoco* **voy.**   *"I don't go (there) either."*

- When words joined by **o... o** or **ni... ni** are the subject of the sentence, the verb can be either singular or plural:

  —**Conduce o Elena o Diego, ¿verdad?**   *"Either Elena or Diego is driving, right?"*

  —**Creo que no quieren conducir ni ella ni él.**   *"I think neither she nor he wants to drive."*

- In Spanish sentences, unlike English ones, two or more negative words may be used:

  Nadie dice nada nunca.   *Nobody ever says anything.*

C. **Que no.** Answer the following questions using **no** and the negative words that correspond to the affirmative ones in the questions. Write dashes for dialogue exchanges.

Modelo   —¿Estás buscando algo?
➤ —No, no estoy buscando nada.

1. —¿Siempre trabajan Uds. los sábados?

   _____

2. —¿Sara asiste a algún espectáculo?

   _____

3. —¿Vas a comprar un traje también?

   _____

4. —¿Uds. están guardando algo en el armario?

   _____

5. —¿Oyes a alguien en la sala?

   _____

6. —¿Pedro y Natalia prueban algunos platos japoneses?

   _____

D. El orden de palabras. Rewrite the following negative sentences. Change the order of the negative words from before the verb to after the verb.

Modelo Ninguno de mis amigos me llama.
> No me llama ninguno de mis amigos.

1. Nadie tiene las llaves del carro.

   _____

2. Ningún médico trabaja en el consultorio ahora.

   _____

3. Patricia nunca viaja por tren.

   _____

4. Ni Carlota ni Eunice usa anteojos.

   _____

5. Nada les interesa.

   _____

6. Nosotros tampoco hablamos con aquellos señores.

   _____

7. A nadie le gustan estas cortinas.

   _____

III. *Saber* and *conocer*

- In Spanish there are two verbs that are equivalent to the English verb *to know:* **saber** and **conocer.** Both these verbs are irregular in the **yo** form but are regular in all the other forms:

	SABER *TO KNOW*		**CONOCER** *TO KNOW*	
	singular	**plural**	**singular**	**plural**
first person	sé	sabemos	**conozco**	conocemos
second person	sabes	sabéis	conoces	conocéis
third person	sabe	saben	conoce	conocen

- **Saber** means to know facts, information, or knowledge that can be stated, such as a name, an address, or a date:

—¿Saben Uds. dónde vive Jacobo?　*"Do you know where Jacobo lives?"*
—Sí, sabemos su dirección.　*"Yes, we know his address."*

E. **¿Qué saben?** Tell the things that people know by writing sentences with **saber.**

Modelo Uds. / el tamaño / la alfombra
➤ Uds. saben el tamaño de la alfombra.

Datos (Information)

la marca *make, brand*	**la talla** *size (articles of clothing)*
el número *size (shoes and gloves)*	**el tamaño** *size; shoe size*
el pronóstico (meteorológico) *weather forecast*	**la videocasetera** *videocassette player*

---

1. Sergio / el número / los zapatos

   _____ sabe _____

2. yo / el título / la novela

   _____ sé _____

3. Ud. / el número de teléfono / el cine

   _____ sabe _____

4. Julia y yo / la talla / el vestido

   _____ sabemos _____

5. Susana y Román / la marca / la videocasetera

   _____ saben _____

6. tú / el pronóstico para mañana

   _____ sabes _____

■ When **saber** is followed directly by an infinitive, it means *to know how* to do something. (See Chapter 3 to review the conjugated verb + infinitive construction.)

—Sabes manejar, ¿no?   *"You know how to drive, don't you?"*
—Un poco, pero no sé estacionar todavía.   *"A little, but I don't know how to park yet."*

F. *Saber* **+ infinitivo.** Tell some of the things that people know how to do. Write sentences using the **saber** + infinitive construction.

Modelo   tú / esquiar ➤ Tú sabes esquiar.

1. yo / reparar carros

   Sé reparar

2. Ud. / cultivar flores

   sabe cultivar

3. Uds. / montar a caballo

   Saben montar

4. Lucía y Verónica / patinar sobre hielo

   saben patinar

5. nosotros / tocar el clarinete

   sabemos tocar

6. Sergio / hacer dibujos animados

   sabe hacer

■ **Conocer** means *to know* a person or *to be familiar* or *acquainted with* a place. The personal **a** must be used with **conocer** when a person is the direct object:

—**Conoces a los señores Durán, ¿verdad?**   "You know Mr. and Mrs. Durán, don't you?"
—**Yo conozco al esposo pero no a la esposa.**   "I know the husband but not the wife."

—**¿Conocen Uds. el país?**   "Are you familiar with the country?"
—**Conocemos la capital y algunas ciudades.**   "We're familiar with the capital and a few cities."

G. En Buenos Aires. Write sentences using the verb **conocer** to say that these tourists are familiar with certain places in Buenos Aires.

Modelo   nosotros / Buenos Aires ➤ Nosotros conocemos Buenos Aires.

1. yo / el Teatro Colón

   Conozco

2. Timoteo / la Plaza de Mayo

   Conoce

➤➤➤➤➤

3. Uds. / La Boca

   conocen

4. tú / la Calle Florida

   conoces

5. Claudia y yo / el subterráneo

   conocemos

6. Ud. / el Café Tango

   conoce

7. Arturo y Julia / muchas confiterías

   conocen

En Buenos Aires

- **Buenos Aires,** the capital of Argentina, has a population of almost 12 million people. It is a modern, dynamic city that has been largely rebuilt since the early 1900s. The heart of the city is the **Plaza de Mayo** where **el Cabildo** (Town Hall), **la Casa Rosada** (Presidential Palace), and **la Municipalidad** (City Hall) are found.

- North of the **Plaza de Mayo** is the traditional shopping area known as **la Calle Florida.** People enjoy having a late afternoon snack in one of the many **confiterías** (tea rooms) in this bustling area.

- **La Boca** is a picturesque old port district south of the city. It was here that Pedro de Mendoza, the Spanish conquistador, founded Buenos Aires in 1536. The neighborhood remains largely Italian. In Buenos Aires, Italian influence is very strong due to the large percentage of inhabitants of Italian background.

- **El Teatro Colón** is one of the world's great opera houses and is the home of Argentina's national orchestra.

- **El subte,** short for **subterráneo,** is the Buenos Aires subway system. It is the oldest subway system in South America.

- **El tango** is perhaps the cultural feature most associated with Buenos Aires and Argentina. The tango began as a dance just before the turn of the twentieth century. **Tango** refers to the song and type of music, as well as the dance. The typical tango orchestra consists of violins, flutes, and the **bandoneón** (concertina). The Argentinian singer Carlos Gardel, who died in 1935, is perhaps the most famous tango artist.

H. Un partido de fútbol. Tell about a soccer match by completing each of the following sentences with the correct form of either **saber** or **conocer.** Use the personal **a** where necessary.

Modelo   nosotros / el portero ➢ Nosotros conocemos al portero.

El fútbol (Soccer)

el arquero *goaltender*	**el portero** *goaltender*
marcar un gol *to score a goal*	**el técnico** *manager, trainer*

---

1. yo / que los jugadores del equipo Azul son excelentes

   _____ *sé* _____

2. Antonio / no / este campo de juego

   _____ *conoce* _____

3. Uds. / el arquero del equipo Amarillo

   _____ *conocen al* _____

4. nosotros / que Pelayo va a marcar unos goles

   _____ *sabemos* _____

5. tú / no / la nacionalidad de Mejía

   _____ *sabes* _____

6. Jorge y Paco / el técnico del equipo Azul

   _____ *conocen al* _____

IV. Question Formation

Yes/no questions

■ Questions that expect yes or no as an answer are called *yes/no questions.* In Spanish, statements can be made into yes/no questions in one of two ways: (1) by inverting the subject and the verb, and (2) by changing your intonation from falling to rising at the end of the sentence without changing the word order:

¿Perfecciona Daniel su español? ⎫
¿Daniel perfecciona su español? ⎭   *Is Daniel improving his Spanish?*

■ The subject can be placed at the end of the question for emphasis:

¿Lee Celia una novela?   *Is Celia reading a novel?*
                                                  (focus on novel)

¿Lee una novela Celia?   *Is Celia reading a novel?*
                                                  (focus on Celia)

■ Statements that consist of a subject, **ser** or **estar,** and an adjective or adverb are usually made into yes/no questions by placing the subject at the end of the sentence, not right after the verb as in English:

El libro es cómico.   *The book is funny.*
¿Es cómico el libro?   *Is the book funny?*

La taquilla está abierta.   *The box office is open.*
¿Está abierta la taquilla?   *Is the box office open?*

■ Statements can be changed into yes/no questions by the addition of phrases called *tags,* such as **¿verdad?, ¿no es verdad?, ¿no?,** and **¿no es cierto?** Tag questions expect the answer yes:

Trotas todos los días, ¿no?   *You jog every day, don't you?*

■ If the statement is negative, only **¿verdad?** can be used as a tag:

No trotas todos los días, ¿verdad?   *You don't jog every day, do you?*

I. Preguntas generales *(Yes/no questions).* Change the following statements into yes/no questions. Place the subject right after the verb.

Modelo   Bárbara lava la ropa. ➤ ¿Lava Bárbara la ropa?

En la oficina (In the office)

el fichero *filing cabinet*

pulsar *to click (a mouse)*

el ratón *mouse (for computer)*

---

1. Ud. prefiere esta marca de cámara.

    _____

2. Los hombres de negocios terminan el informe hoy.

    _____

3. La cliente pide más informes.

    _____

4. Tú abres el fichero.

_____

5. José está trabajando en la computadora.

_____

6. Uds. pulsan el ratón.

_____

J. **¿_Ser_ o _estar_ + adjetivo o adverbio + sujeto?** Change the following statements into yes/no questions. Use the formula in the title of this exercise.

Modelo   Los alumnos son trabajadores.
   ➤ ¿Son trabajadores los alumnos?

1. La costa es larga.

_____

2. Los gemelos son muy traviesos.

_____

3. El bosque nacional está cerca.

_____

4. El correo electrónico es útil.

_____

5. Sus sobrinos están acatarrados.

_____

6. El salmón está sabroso.

_____

Interrogative words in information questions

■ Information questions begin with an interrogative word such as **¿Qué?**
They expect some information as a response:

¿Qué quieres hacer?   *What do you want to do?*

■ Prepositions must always precede the interrogative words in Spanish. They
cannot be placed at the end of the sentence as they often are in English:

¿De dónde regresan?   *Where are they returning from?*

■ The most important interrogative words:

¿cómo? *how?*	**¿cuál?, ¿cuáles?** *which one(s)?*
¿cuándo? *when?*	**¿qué?** *what?, which?*
¿dónde? *where? (at what place?)*	**¿por qué?** *why?*
¿adónde? *where? (to what place?)*	**¿para qué?** *for what purpose?*
¿de dónde? *from where?*	**¿quién?, ¿quiénes?** *who? (subject)*
¿cuánto?, ¿cuánta? *how much?*	**¿a quién?, ¿a quiénes?** *whom? (object)*
¿cuántos?, ¿cuántas? *how many?*	**¿de quién?, ¿de quiénes?** *whose?*

Notes:

1. **¿Dónde?** is used to ask about location. **¿Adónde?** is used with verbs of
motion and asks direction:

   ¿Dónde viven los Linares?   *Where do the Linareses live?*
   ¿Adónde va María Luisa?   *Where is María Luisa going?*

2. **¿Cuál?** and **¿Cuáles?** are often replaced by **¿Qué?** before a noun:

   ¿Qué videojuegos tienes?   *Which videogames do you have?*

   ¿Cuál? is used to mean *What?* when an identification is asked for:

   ¿Cuál es el título del libro?   *What's the title of the book?*

3. **¿Qué?** before the verb **ser** asks for a definition:

   ¿Qué es antropología?   *What is anthropology?*

4. By itself, **¿Cómo?** is used to ask for repetition of something the listener
didn't understand or hear or to express surprise at something the listener
heard:

   —**La clase comienza a las ocho.**   *"The class begins at 8:00."*
   —**¿Cómo?**   *"What?"*

   ¿Cómo? has different meanings that depend on whether it is used with **ser**
or **estar:**

   ¿Cómo está Roberto?   *How is Roberto? (asks about health)*
   ¿Cómo es Roberto?   *What does Roberto look like? /*
                                          What is Roberto like?

K. Para formar preguntas. Write the information questions that are asked to produce the following statements. The underlined words tell you the information requested.

Modelo   El profesor prepara <u>una conferencia</u>. ➤ ¿Qué prepara el profesor?

1. Voy a <u>la tienda de comestibles</u>.

   _____

2. Carmen vuelve <u>el martes</u>.

   _____

3. Compramos <u>cuatro</u> pares de zapatos.

   _____

4. Debes ahorrar <u>mucha</u> plata.

   _____

5. Concha y Narciso viajan <u>en barco</u>.

   _____

6. Llego del <u>centro comercial</u>.

   _____

L. Una conversación. Because you hear only one side of a conversation, you must guess what the other person asked to get such a response. Write the information questions that were asked. (Note that the information requested is underlined.)

Modelo   ➤ —¿Qué traen?
               —Traemos <u>bombones</u>.

1. — _____

   —Voy al <u>acuario</u>.

2. — _____

   —El collar es de <u>oro y plata</u>.

3. — _____

   —Los Arroyo tienen <u>ocho</u> hoteles.

4. — _____

   —Bucean <u>con mucho cuidado</u>.

➤➤➤➤➤

5. —_____

—Estos regalos son para <u>los gemelos</u>.

6. —_____

—La reunión comienza <u>a las tres</u>.

M. Preguntas personales. Answer the following questions in complete Spanish sentences.

1. ¿A quiénes ves todos los días? ¿A quiénes no ves con frecuencia?

_____

2. ¿Con quiénes pasas los fines de semana?

_____

3. ¿Qué cosas sabes hacer bien?

_____

4. ¿Eres aficionado o aficionada al fútbol? Si juegas al fútbol, ¿cómo juegas?

_____

5. ¿Qué países y ciudades quieres conocer?

_____

N. Composición. Write a dialogue of eight to ten exchanges between two people. One person asks questions to find out about someone; the other person answers. The people involved may be real or imaginary.

Adjectives

- In Spanish, adjectives agree in gender and number with the nouns they modify. Adjectives with a masculine singular form that ends in -**o** replace it with an -**a** to form the feminine and add an -**s** to form the plural. These adjectives have four forms:

CUIDADOSO *CAREFUL*

	masculine	feminine
singular	cuidadoso	cuidadosa
plural	cuidadosos	cuidadosas

Note: Many adjectives with four forms are actually past participles (see Chapter 17 on past participles as adjectives). When functioning as adjectives, these participles agree with the noun in gender and number:

El médico es un hombre dedicado.	*The doctor is a dedicated man.*
Los jugadores están cansados.	*The players are tired.*
La ópera es muy divertida.	*The opera is very amusing.*
Estas niñas son bailarinas cumplidas.	*These girls are accomplished dancers.*

- Adjectives with a masculine singular form that ends in a consonant or -**e** do not change in the feminine form. These adjectives have only two forms, a singular and a plural:

	FÁCIL *EASY*	GRANDE *BIG*
	masculine and feminine	**masculine and feminine**
singular	fácil	grande
plural	fáciles	grandes

- Adjectives that end in the suffixes -**dor,** -**ón,** and -**án** add an -**a** to form the feminine. These adjectives add -**es,** instead of -**os,** to form the masculine plural:

TRABAJADOR *HARD-WORKING*

	masculine	feminine
singular	trabajador	trabajadora
plural	trabajadores	trabajadoras

COMILÓN *GLUTTONOUS*

	masculine	feminine
singular	comilón	comilona
plural	comilones	comilonas

■ In Spanish, descriptive adjectives usually follow the nouns they modify; in English, all adjectives precede the nouns they modify:

Es un hombre orgulloso.	*He's a proud man.*
Tienen ideas geniales.	*They have brilliant ideas.*

■ Adjectives that express quantity precede the noun: **mucho, poco, bastante, suficiente, cuánto, varios, ambos** *(both):*

Paco Oñate gana bastante plata.	*Paco Oñate earns quite a lot of money.*
Hace muchos años que viven aquí.	*They've been living here for many years.*

■ Adjectives can be modified by adverbs such as **más, tan,** and **muy:**

Esta calle es tan ruidosa.	*This street is so noisy.*
Este cuarto es muy bonito.	*This room is very pretty.*

■ In exclamations with **¡Qué!**, the adjective usually follows the noun:

¡Qué calle más ruidosa!	*What a noisy street!*
¡Qué cuarto tan bonito!	*What a pretty room!*

■ Certain adjectives lose their final -**o** before a masculine singular noun: **uno, bueno, malo, primero, tercero, alguno,** and **ninguno. (Alguno** and **ninguno** add an accent mark when they are shortened to **algún** and **ningún.**)

—¿Sirven unos pasteles?	*"Are they serving some pastries?"*
—No queda ningún pastel.	*"There isn't a single pastry left."*
Es un buen día para pasear.	*It's a good day to go for a walk.*

■ The adjectives **grande** and **cualquiera** *(any)* are shortened to **gran** and **cualquier,** respectively, before any singular noun:

—Cualquier novela de Vargas es excelente.	*"Any novel by Vargas is excellent."*
—Es cierto. Es un gran autor.	*"It's true. He's a great author."*

■ Some Spanish adjectives have different meanings that depend on whether they precede or follow the nouns they modify:

un gran jugador *a great player*	un pobre hombre *a poor man (unfortunate)*
un jugador grande *a big player*	un hombre pobre *a poor man (without money)*
el mismo médico *the same doctor*	la única persona *the only person*
el médico mismo *the doctor himself*	una persona única *a unique person*

- Adjectives that modify two plural nouns of the same gender are in the plural of that gender:

Venden trajes y abrigos caros.	*They sell expensive suits and overcoats.*
Ponen alfombras y cortinas blancas.	*They're putting in white rugs and curtains.*

- If two nouns of different genders, whether singular or plural, are modified by a single adjective, the adjective is masculine plural:

Elena busca un vestido y una falda baratos.	*Elena is looking for an inexpensive dress and skirt.*
Vamos a visitar los templos y las iglesias antiguos.	*We're going to visit the old temples and churches.*

- If two adjectives modify a noun, they both follow it and are joined by **y**:

Leti es una niña dulce y cariñosa.	*Leti is a sweet, loving child.*
Es un juego divertido y complicado.	*It's an amusing, complicated game.*

A. Adjetivos. Complete the following list by filling in the correct form of the adjective in parentheses.

noun	adjective
1. cajón	_____ (vacío)
2. sopa	_____ (salado)
3. mapas	_____ (viejo)
4. personas	_____ (cortés)
5. enfermedad	_____ (grave)
6. exámenes	_____ (difícil)
7. calles	_____ (resbaloso)
8. vacaciones	_____ (inolvidable)
9. tarde	_____ (oscuro)
10. escritora	_____ (conocido)
11. legumbres	_____ (congelado)
12. muchacho	_____ (formal)
13. jugadores	_____ (feliz)
14. zapatos	_____ (elegante)
15. habitación	_____ (cómodo)

B. En plural. Write the correct form of the adjective in parentheses for each pair of nouns.

Modelo   un periódico y una revista (bueno) ➤ buenos

1. un veterinario y una contable (casado)   _____

2. rosas y tulipanes (hermoso)   _____

3. una pulsera y un collar (costoso)   _____

4. la madre y los hijos (cariñoso)   _____

5. días y noches (formidable)   _____

6. científicos y políticos (idealista)   _____

7. salmón y langosta (rico)   _____

8. sala y habitación (amueblado)   _____

C. ¿Dónde colocas el adjetivo? Complete each of the following sentences by writing the adjective in the correct space. Make sure the adjective agrees with its noun.

1. Hay _____ revistas _____ en la mesita. (alguno)

2. ¡Qué _____ plato tan _____! (sabroso)

3. Piensan tomar una clase de _____ literatura

   _____. (moderno)

4. Ya es el _____ día _____ del semestre. (tercero)

5. Creen que Granados es un _____ compositor

   _____. (grande)

6. Leonora es una _____ mujer _____. (único)

7. Los Lorca prefieren las _____ costumbres

   _____. (tradicional)

8. Isidoro y Tomás van al _____ médico _____.
   (mismo)

9. Les encanta la _____ poesía _____. (romántico)

10. Lucas es programador y gana _____ dinero

    _____. (bastante)

D. ¿Cómo son? Tell what Alicia thinks of her friends and family members. Write sentences with the verb **ser** and the adjectives given.

Modelo   Rita: tímido / sincero ➤ Rita es tímida y sincera.

> ### Algunos adjetivos
>
> **comprensivo** *understanding*
> **formal** *serious; reliable*
> **sensible** *sensitive*

1. mis abuelos: comprensivo / formal

   _____

2. Roberto: sensible / valiente

   _____

3. tú *(fem.):* intelectual / encantador

   _____

4. mis sobrinas: travieso / tonto

   _____

5. Uds. *(masc.):* ambicioso / discreto

   _____

6. Cristóbal: pesimista / cuidadoso

   _____

E. ¿Cómo son? Tell what these people look like. Write sentences with the adjectives given and the verb **ser.**

Modelos   Vera: bajo / pequeño ➤ Vera es baja y pequeña.
yo *(masc.):* flaco / débil ➤ Yo soy flaco y débil.

1. Magdalena y Jaime: alto / guapo

   _____

2. José Armando, tú: delgado / moreno

   _____

➤➤➤➤➤

3. los bebés: gordito / pequeñito

_____

4. nosotros: joven / rubio

_____

5. chicas, Uds.: grande / bonito

_____

6. Martita: pelirrojo / hermoso

_____

F. ¿Qué hace juego con...? *(What goes with . . . ?)* Some friends are talking about the colors of some clothes that match or don't match others. Fill in the correct form of each adjective.

Modelo La bufanda _amarilla_ hace juego con el vestido _anaranjado_.
(amarillo / anaranjado)

1. La corbata _____ hace juego con la camisa

_____. (rojo / blanco)

2. Los pantalones _____ no hacen juego con la chaqueta

_____. (negro / verde)

3. Las camisetas _____ hacen juego con los jeans

_____. (gris / marrón)

4. El suéter _____ no hace juego con la falda

_____. (rosado / morado)

5. La blusa _____ hace juego con el traje _____.
(azul / café)

6. Las zapatillas _____ no hacen juego con las medias

_____. (anaranjado / verde)

Adjectives of nationality

■ Adjectives of nationality that end in -o in the masculine singular have the regular four forms:

ARGENTINO *ARGENTINIAN*

	masculine	feminine
singular	argentino	argentina
plural	argentinos	argentinas

■ Adjectives of nationality that end in a consonant also have four forms. However, the masculine plural ends in -es, instead of -os. Adjectives of nationality that have an accent mark on the last syllable of the masculine singular form lose that accent mark when an ending is added:

ESPAÑOL *SPANISH*

	masculine	feminine
singular	español	española
plural	españoles	españolas

INGLÉS *ENGLISH*

	masculine	feminine
singular	inglés	inglesa
plural	ingleses	inglesas

Note: The masculine singular form of the adjective of nationality is the same form as the name of the language: **el español** *(Spanish)*, **el inglés** *(English)*, **el alemán** *(German)*, **el francés** *(French)*.

G. Adjetivos de nacionalidad. Complete the following list by writing in the missing forms of the adjectives of nationality.

masc. sing.	masc. pl.	fem. sing.	fem. pl.
1. suizo	_____	_____	_____
2. _____	_____	_____	japonesas
3. _____	franceses	_____	_____
4. _____	_____	italiana	_____
5. alemán	_____	_____	_____
6. _____	_____	_____	chinas

H. Nacionalidad y origen. Write two sentences to state the nationality and background of these Latin American people.

Modelo   Fabián Soria: Chile / Inglaterra
   ➤ Fabián Soria es chileno. Es de origen inglés.

1. Julio y Carmen Betanzos: Argentina / Rusia

_____

2. Maximiliano Valverde: Brasil / Portugal

_____

3. Beatriz Álvarez: Costa Rica / Grecia

_____

4. Liliana Serrano y yo *(fem.):* Venezuela / Irlanda

_____

5. tú *(masc.):* Cuba / África

_____

6. yo *(fem.):* Perú / España

_____

La moneda

- The European Union has officially endorsed the euro as the currency of its member nations. The euro bills and coins will be put into circulation by the year 2002. However, the Latin American countries that belong to the Latin American Free Trade Association, **MERCOSUR (Mercado Común Sudamericano), el Mercado Común Centroamericano,** and the **Pacto Andino,** show no sign of giving up their national currencies.
- The following are names of some Latin American currencies: Bolivia, **el boliviano;** Ecuador, **el sucre;** Guatemala, **el quetzal;** Honduras, **el lempira;** Nicaragua, **el córdoba;** Paraguay, **el guaraní;** Peru, **el sol;** Venezuela, **el bolívar.** The currency of Argentina, Chile, Colombia, Mexico, and Uruguay is **el peso;** and the currency of Costa Rica and El Salvador is **el colón.** Note that even though some currencies share the same name, their value differs on the world market.

I. **Preguntas personales.** Answer the following questions in complete Spanish sentences.

1. ¿Cómo es tu mejor amigo o amiga? (Usa dos adjetivos.)

_____

2. ¿Cómo es el actor o la actriz que te gusta más?

_____

3. ¿De qué origen eres?

_____

4. ¿Qué colores prefieres para un carro (la ropa / los muebles / tu cuarto)?

_____

5. ¿Cómo son las personas que más respetas?

_____

J. **Composición.** Write a composition of eight sentences in which you describe a special person in your life. Tell about his or her background and physical, character, and personality traits.

monstrative Adjectives; Possessive
ectives; Adjectives as Pronouns

nstrative Adjectives

re are three demonstrative adjectives in Spanish: **este** (*this*; near the
...ker), **ese** (*that*; near the person spoken to), and **aquel** (*that*; far from
both the speaker and the person spoken to). A demonstrative adjective
agrees in gender and number with the noun it modifies:

ESTE *THIS*

	masculine	feminine
singular	este	esta
plural	estos	estas

ESE *THAT*

	masculine	feminine
singular	ese	esa
plural	esos	esas

AQUEL *THAT*

	masculine	feminine
singular	aquel	aquella
plural	aquellos	aquellas

—¿Me dejas ver esa revista?   *"Will you let me see that magazine?"*
—Cómo no. Esta revista es muy   *"Of course. This magazine is very*
  linda.   *beautiful."*

—¿Qué es aquel rascacielos?   *"What is that skyscraper (over there)?"*

—Aquel edificio es el hotel   *"That building (over there) is the*
  Maravillas.   *Maravillas Hotel."*

A. *Este, ese, aquel.* Complete the list by writing the demonstrative adjective
you would use with each noun.

	this/these	that/those	that/those (over there)
1. el cine	este/estos	ese/esos	aquel/aquellas
2. la taquilla	esta/estas	esa/esas	aquella/aquellas
3. los carteles	estos	esos	aquellos
4. las carteras	estas	esas	aquellas
5. el reloj	este	ese	aquel

6. los contables   _estos_   _esas_   _aquellos_

7. las paredes   _estas_   _esas_   _aquellas_

8. la habitación   _esta_   _esa_   _aquella_

9. el periodista   _este_   _ese_   _aquel_

10. la mermelada   _esta_   _esa_   _aquella_

B. En el centro comercial. As you and your friend walk through the shopping center, you comment on the things you see. Express the English demonstrative adjectives in Spanish, using the correct form of *este* or *ese*.

El centro comercial

descompuesto *broken, out of order*   **el puesto** *stand, small shop*

la escalera mecánica *escalator*   **la sucursal** *branch (of store, business)*

---

1. *(This)* _este_ centro comercial es muy grande.

2. *(That)* _ese_ almacén es nuevo.

3. *(These)* _estas_ tiendas están abiertas hasta las diez.

4. Podemos comer algo en uno de *(those)* _esas_ cafés.

5. *(That)* _esa_ sucursal no tiene cosas para la casa.

6. *(Those)* _esas_ tiendas de discos tienen muchos discos compactos.

7. *(This)* _esta_ escalera mecánica está descompuesta.

8. Vamos a ver lo que venden en *(these)* _estos_ puestos.

C. Regalos. You are at the mall shopping for gifts for your family and friends. Write dialogues in which the salesperson asks if you want this/these . . . , and you respond by saying no, you want that/those . . . (over there). Practice using the forms of **este** and **aquel**. Write dashes for dialogue exchanges.

Modelo   querer / pluma
         DEPENDIENTE: —¿Quiere Ud. esta pluma?
         CLIENTE: —No, quiero aquella pluma.

1. querer comprar / guantes

DEPENDIENTE: _Quiere comprar ud. estos guantes?_

CLIENTE: _Quiero comprar aquellos guantes_

>>>>>>

2. preferir / caja de bombones

   DEPENDIENTE: _prefiere esta caja_

   CLIENTE: _prefiero aquella caja_

3. comprar / juguete

   DEPENDIENTE: _compra este juguete_

   CLIENTE: _compro aquel juguete_

4. querer ver / bufandas

   DEPENDIENTE: _quiere ver estas bufandas_

   CLIENTE: _quiero ver aquellas_

5. preferir / anillo

   DEPENDIENTE: _prefiere este_

   CLIENTE: _prefiero aquel_

6. desear regalar / raqueta de tenis

   DEPENDIENTE: _desea regalar esta_

   CLIENTE: _deseo regalar aquella_

D. *¿Este, ese o aquel?* The salesclerk needs to find out which item(s) you want to see. Write the clerk's question using the correct forms of the demonstrative adjectives in parentheses.

Modelo   —¿Me enseña el libro de poemas? (este / ese)
   ➤ —¿Cuál? ¿Este libro o ese libro?

1. —¿Me enseña los mapas? (este / aquel)

   — _estos aquellos_

2. —¿Me enseña el disco? (ese / aquel)

   — _ese aquel_

3. —¿Me enseña el átlas? (este / ese)

   — _este o ese_

4. —¿Me enseña las revistas? (este / ese)

— _estas   esas_

5. —¿Me enseña la biografía de Chávez? (ese / aquel)

— _esa   aquella_

6. —¿Me enseña las tarjetas? (este / aquel)

— _estas   aquellas_

II. Possessive Adjectives

■ Possessive adjectives are pronouns that function as adjectives. They agree with the nouns they modify:

(yo) **mi / mis**	(nosotros) **nuestro / nuestra / nuestros / nuestras**
(tú) **tu / tus**	(vosotros) **vuestro / vuestra / vuestros / vuestras**
(él, ella, Ud.) **su / sus**	(ellos, ellas, Uds.) **su / sus**

■ **Mi, tu,** and **su** have two forms each, a singular and a plural. **Nuestro** and **vuestro** have four forms each, like any adjective that ends in -o.

—¿Quieres ver mi nueva pulsera?   *"Do you want to see my new bracelet?"*

—Ah sí, y tus pendientes también.   *"Oh, yes, and your earrings too."*

—¿De dónde son sus primos?   *"Where are your cousins from?"*

—Nuestro primo es italiano y nuestra prima es colombiana.   *"Our male cousin is Italian and our female cousin is Colombian."*

■ The possessive adjective **su (sus)** means *his, her, its, your,* and *their.* To clarify who is referred to, replace **su/sus** with the definite article (and noun) and add a phrase consisting of **de** + pronoun:

—Aquí vienen Marcos y Sandra. Voy a pedir prestado su videojuego.   *"Here come Marcos and Sandra. I'm going to borrow his/her/their videogame."*

—¿El (videojuego) de él o el (videojuego) de ella?   *"His videogame or her videogame?"*

E. ¿De quién es? Tell to whom each item belongs. Write phrases using the possessive adjectives.

Modelo   el gorro / (él) ➤ su gorro

1. la motocicleta / (ellos)   _su motocicleta._

2. el peine / (tú)   _tu peine_

3. los lentes de contacto / (ella)   _sus lentes de contacto_

➤➤➤➤➤

4. el perro / (él)   _Su_

5. las tijeras / (yo)   _mis_

6. el monedero / (Uds.)   _Su_

F. La familia. Clara Inés is talking about her family. Complete the sentences by filling in the possessive adjectives based on the cues in English.

Modelo   _Mi_ *(My)* familia es muy unida.

La familia

casado *married*	**los gemelos** *twins*
el cuñado *brother-in-law*	**el marido** *husband*
la cuñada *sister-in-law*	**unido** *close*

---

1. ____*mi*____ *(My)* hermano Roberto está casado.

2. ____*Su*____ *(His)* esposa se llama Laura.

3. ____*Su*____ *(Their)* hijo se llama Daniel.

4. ____*mi*____ *(My)* hermana Sara está casada también.

5. ____*Su*____ *(Her)* marido Paul es inglés.

6. ____*Su*____ *(Their)* gemelos tienen cuatro años.

7. ____*mis*____ *(My)* cuñados son muy simpáticos.

8. ____*mis*____ *(My)* sobrinos son cariñosos y graciosos.

9. __*nuestros*__*(Our)* padres nos quieren mucho.

10. __*nuestra*__ *(Our)* mamá espera tener muchos nietos.

G. ¿Con quién(es)? Tell with whom people do certain things. Write sentences using possessive adjectives.

Modelo   Uds. / practicar francés / tía
             ➤ Uds. practican francés con su tía.

Gente y actividades

el empleado *employee*	**los naipes** *playing cards*
el jefe *boss*	**la reunión** *meeting*

---

1. tú / cenar / padres

   tú cenas con tus padres

2. los empleados / tener una reunión / jefe

   los empleados tienen una reunión con su jefe

3. Claudia y yo / esperar el autobús / amigos

   Claudia y yo esperamos el autobús con nuestros amigos

4. yo / ir al concierto / novio

   Yo voy al concierto con mi novio

5. Daniel y Raquel / jugar a los naipes / hermanos

   Daniel y Raquel juegan a los naipes con sus hermanos

6. Ud. / visitar la finca / abuelos

   Ud. visita la finca con sus abuelos

H. ¡Qué gentío! *(What a lot of people!)* It's difficult to find relatives and friends in the crowded train station. Find these people and point them out. Use possessive adjectives and the cues in parentheses in your responses.

Modelo —¿Dónde está la amiga de Julia? (en la puerta)
➤ —Su amiga está en la puerta.

La estación de tren

el andén *platform*
el horario *timetable*
la puerta *gate*

---

1. —¿Dónde está el cuñado de Marisol? (cerca del quiosco)

   — Su cuñado está cerca del quiosco

2. —¿Dónde están los nietos de los señores Bergamín? (en el andén)

   — Sus nietos están en el andén

3. —Paquita, ¿dónde está tu abuela? (en la puerta)

   — mi abuela está en la puerta

➤➤➤➤➤

4. —¿Dónde está la sobrina de doña Josefa? (en la taquilla)

   — _Su sobrina está en la taquilla_

5. —Señores, ¿dónde está su nieto? (en la escalera mecánica)

   — _Mi nieto está en ..._

6. —Pedro y Silvia, ¿dónde está su tía? (leyendo el horario)

   — _nuestra tía está leyendo el ..._

Los trenes

RENFE (Red Nacional de los Ferrocarriles Españoles), which stands for *Spanish National Railroad Network,* is responsible for the administration of Spain's railroads. In spite of the reduction in passenger and freight service over the years because of increased road transportation, RENFE has successfully undertaken vast renovation programs. The **AVE (Tren de Alta Velocidad),** the high-speed train that runs from Madrid to Sevilla in less than three hours, is very popular and profitable, as is the **auto-expreso,** the Motorail train that connects some of the big Spanish cities with the coastal areas. Renovation of the Spanish railroad system has also made travel to the rest of Europe much easier and has promoted international traffic.

III. Adjectives as Pronouns

■ Pronouns are used to replace nouns. Adjectives in Spanish can be used as pronouns when the noun they modify is deleted: **el coche verde ➤ el verde; los coches verdes ➤ los verdes.** In English, we would say *the green one* or *the green ones:*

—La bicicleta azul es más ligera que *la roja.*

—Pero la bicicleta roja tiene mejores frenos que *la azul.*

—Los zapatos nuevos son más bonitos que *los viejos.*

—Es cierto. Pero los viejos son más cómodos que *los nuevos.*

"The blue bicycle is lighter than the red one."

"But the red bicycle has better brakes than the blue one."

"The new shoes are prettier than the old ones."

"That's true. But the old ones are more comfortable than the new ones."

I. **De adjetivo a pronombre (*From adjective to pronoun*).** Rewrite each of the following phrases by changing the adjective to a pronoun.

1. la computadora cara   _la cara_

2. los pasteles congelados   _los congelados_

3. el estéreo descompuesto   _el descompuesto_

4. las estudiantes francesas   _las francesas_

5. los vasos llenos   _los llenos_

6. el apartamento amueblado   _el amueblado_

7. la prueba fácil   _la fácil_

8. las personas comprensivas   _las comprensivas_

9. los alimentos nutritivos   _los nutritivos_

10. el chico pelirrojo   _el pel_

J. ¿Cuál prefieres? You are asked which of two things you prefer. Write both possible answers, but use the adjective as a pronoun in each one.

Modelo   ¿Cuál prefieres, la camisa blanca o la camisa amarilla?
    ➤ Prefiero la blanca. / Prefiero la amarilla.

1. ¿Cuál prefieres, la música clásica o la música popular?

Prefiero la clásica / la popular

2. ¿Cuáles prefieres ver, los programas serios o los programas cómicos?

los serios / los cómicos

3. ¿Cuáles prefieres ver, las películas estadounidenses o las películas extranjeras?

las estadounidenses / las extranjeras

4. ¿Dónde quieres comer, en el restaurante italiano o en el restaurante mexicano?

el italiano / el mexicano

5. ¿Dónde quieres vivir, en la ciudad grande o en la ciudad pequeña?

la grande / la pequeña

6. ¿A quiénes prefieres conocer, a los chicos intelectuales o a los chicos atléticos?

los intelectuales / los atléticos

7. ¿Cuáles prefieres, los platos dulces o los platos salados?

los dulces / los salados

K. Preguntas personales. Answer the following questions in complete Spanish sentences.

1. ¿Cuáles prefieres, las canciones populares o las folklóricas?

   _____

2. ¿Cómo son tus amigos? ¿Quién es el/la intelectual, el/la optimista, el/la idealista, el/la paciente, el/la sensible?

   _____

   _____

3. ¿Cuál prefieres comer, la comida china o la japonesa?

   _____

4. ¿Cuáles son las cosas favoritas de tu mejor amigo? ¿Cuáles son tus cosas favoritas?

   _____

   _____

5. ¿Aprendes más en las clases difíciles o en las fáciles? ¿Por qué?

   _____

L. Composición. Write a composition of eight sentences about the members of your family. Describe their relationship to you and where they live or what they do. Use as many demonstrative and possessive adjectives as possible.

Adverbs; Comparative Constructions; Superlative Constructions and the Absolute Superlative (-ísimo)

I. Adverbs

The formation and kinds of adverbs

- Adverbs are words or phrases that modify verbs, adjectives, and sometimes other adverbs. In Spanish, adverbs are formed by adding the suffix -**mente** (-*ly* in English) to the distinct feminine form of the adjective:

directo *direct*	**directamente** *directly*
económico *economical*	**económicamente** *economically*

- To form adverbs from adjectives that do not have a distinct feminine form, -**mente** is added to the masculine/feminine singular:

dulce *sweet*	**dulcemente** *sweetly*
fácil *easy*	**fácilmente** *easily*

- Some commonly used adverbs that end in -**mente:**

completamente *completely*	**perfectamente** *perfectly*
finalmente *finally*	**posiblemente** *possibly*
frecuentemente *frequently*	**probablemente** *probably*
generalmente *generally*	**verdaderamente** *truly, really*

- Some adverbs have an irregular form or are identical to their corresponding adjective:

bueno *good*	**bien** *well*
malo *bad*	**mal** *badly*
mejor *better*	**mejor** *better*
peor *worse*	**peor** *worse*

- The following adverbs are grouped by function. There are too many adverbs and adverbial phrases to list here; however, some phrases can be changed to make others. For example, **el año pasado** can be changed to make **el mes pasado** or **la semana pasada.**

ADVERBS OF QUANTITY
(adverbs and adverbial phrases that tell how much):

demasiado *too much*	**mucho** *a lot*
más *more*	**poco** *little*
menos *less*	**tanto** *so much*

ADVERBS OF TIME (adverbs and adverbial phrases that tell when):

ahora *now*

ahora mismo *right now*

antes *before*

después *afterward*

el año próximo/pasado *next/last year*

en este momento *at this moment*

en seguida *right away, immediately*

este año *this year*

hoy *today*

luego *then, afterwards*

mañana (por la mañana)
  tomorrow (morning)

por la tarde *in the afternoon*

todavía *still*

todavía no *not yet*

ya *already, now*

ya no *no longer*

ADVERBS OF FREQUENCY
(adverbs and adverbial phrases that show how often):

a menudo; muchas veces *often*

a veces *sometimes*

de vez en cuando *from time to time*

nunca *never*

otra vez *again*

siempre *always*

todos los días *every day*

ADVERBS OF LOCATION
(adverbs and adverbial phrases that tell where; many are similar to prepositions):

abajo *down, downstairs*

allá *over there*

allí *there*

al fondo *in back, at the bottom*

al lado (de) *beside, next door, next (to), close (to)*

a la derecha/izquierda (de) *on/to the right/left (of)*

aquí *here*

arriba *up, upstairs*

atrás *in back*

cerca (de) *near, nearby, close to*

delante (de) *in front (of)*

detrás (de) *behind, in back (of)*

entre *between, among*

enfrente (de) *opposite, across (from)*

lejos (de) *far away, far (from)*

por algún sitio/lado *somewhere*

por ningún sitio/lado *nowhere*

A. Adverbios. Write the adverb ending in **-mente** that corresponds to each of the following adjectives.

Modelo típico ➤ típicamente

1. generoso _____

2. amable _____

3. difícil _____

4. profundo _____

5. fuerte _____

6. peligroso _____

7. afortunado _____

8. maravilloso _____

B. ¿Dónde y cuándo? Complete the following sentences by writing in the missing adverbs, adverbial phrases, or prepositions. (Don't forget to use contractions where necessary.)

1. La tienda de videos está _____ *(next to)* la papelería.

2. Mari Carmen va a llegar _____ *(next week)*.

3. La empresa no está _____ *(far from)* el centro.

4. Hay una reunión _____ *(tomorrow afternoon)*.

5. El gato está _____ *(behind)* el sofá.

6. El avión está llegando _____ *(right now)*.

7. El banco queda _____ *(between)* el hotel y la tienda de recuerdos.

8. _____ *(This year)* tomamos seis materias.

C. Frecuentemente. Tell how often people do something by writing in the missing words or phrases.

1. Pedro estudia en la biblioteca _____ *(every day)*.

2. ¿_____ *(Always)* almuerzas a la una?

3. Visitan a sus abuelos _____ *(many times)* al año.

4. Los chicos juegan al fútbol _____ *(from time to time)*.

5. _____ *(Never)* voy a aquel café.

6. ¿Por qué tengo que hacer la tarea _____ *(again)*?

7. No veo a los Sánchez _____ *(often)*.

8. _____ *(Sometimes)* prefieren tomar el autobús.

The placement of adverbs

- Adverbs that tell how something is done (adverbs of manner) are placed right after the verb they modify or as close to the verb as possible:

—¿Cómo patinan Leonora y Memo?   *"How do Leonora and Memo skate?"*
—Ella patina bien. Él patina mal.   *"She skates well. He skates badly."*

- Adverbs that modify adjectives and other adverbs precede the adjective or adverb they modify:

Carmen es *muy* generosa y paciente.   *Carmen is very generous and patient.*

El coro canta *sumamente* bien.   *The chorus sings extremely well.*

El bebé duerme *muy* profundamente.   *The baby is sleeping very soundly.*

- Adverbs cannot be placed between an auxiliary (or helping) verb and the main verb, as they commonly are in English:

Por fin Pedro está terminando el informe.   *Pedro is finally finishing the report.*

- Direct objects often come between the verb and the adverb. These include negative and indefinite words such as **nada** and **algo**:

Isabel escribe cartas frecuentemente.   *Isabel writes letters frequently.*

María no dice nada sinceramente.   *María doesn't say anything sincerely.*

D. Colocar los adverbios. Rearrange the strings of words to make complete sentences. Pay particular attention to the placement of the adverb in each sentence.

Modelo   inútil / este aparato / totalmente / es
➤ Este aparato es totalmente inútil.

1. diligentemente / estudia / muy / Soledad

_____

2. ridículas / completamente / sus ideas / son

_____

3. muy / corren / esos atletas / despacio

_____

4. las preguntas / más / contestas / fácilmente

_____

5. a menudo / los conciertos / muy / asistimos a

_____

6. no / seriamente / nada / Lorenzo / dice

_____

7. Uds. / muy / van a esquiar / este año / poco

_____

■ When two or more adverbs ending in -**mente** modify the same word, the suffix -**mente** is placed only on the last adverb in the series. Note that the form of the adverbs before the final one is feminine (if the adjective has a distinct feminine form):

Berta cuida a los niños _responsable_ **y** _cariñosamente._	_Berta takes care of the children reliably and lovingly._

E. Se hace sencillamente. _(It's done simply.)_ Expand the sentences given by changing the adjectives to adverbs that end in -**mente** and adding them to the sentences. Some sentences will have two adverbs.

Modelo   Susana habla. + constante
➤ Susana habla constantemente.

1. Ud. trabaja. + ambicioso

_____

2. Plácido y María cantan. + hermoso / romántico

_____

3. Tú comes. + rápido

_____

4. Augusta lee. + inteligente / diligente

_____

5. Yo dibujo. + horrible

_____

6. Uds. juegan. + valiente / orgulloso

_____

■ Adverbs that end in -**mente** can be replaced by the preposition **con** + the corresponding noun:

cuidadosamente = **con cuidado**

frecuentemente = **con frecuencia**

rápidamente = **con rapidez**

F. **Convertir las frases** *(Changing the phrases).* Write the adverb ending in -**mente** that corresponds to the phrase of **con** + noun.

1. con elegancia _____

2. con timidez _____

3. con alegría _____

4. con generosidad _____

5. con seguridad _____

6. con paciencia _____

7. con perfección _____

8. con debilidad _____

■ There are several adverbs and adverbial phrases that indicate when something happened in the past. (You may wish to review the preterit tense in Chapter 13.) Study the following past time expressions:

anoche *last night*   **ayer por la mañana** *yesterday morning*

ayer *yesterday*   **la semana pasada** *last week*

anteayer *the day before yesterday*

G. **¿Presente o pasado?** Underline the correct adverb or adverbial phrase given in parentheses for each sentence. The context of the sentence and the tense of the verb will help you choose the correct adverb.

Modelo   Los alumnos estudiaron (mañana / ayer).

1. Estamos pensando en hacer un viaje a Cartagena (el mes próximo / el año pasado).

2. Todos caminaron a la heladería (mañana / anoche).

3. Juan navegó en el web (ayer por la tarde / ahora mismo).

4. Sus parientes llegan (pasado mañana / el sábado pasado).

5. ¿Guardaste los regalos (en este momento / ayer)?

6. Palomita lo pasó muy bien (el fin de semana pasado / el domingo próximo).

7. Saco libros de la biblioteca (anteayer / después).

8. Alicia y Benito van a regresar de la capital (la semana próxima / la semana pasada).

Cartagena

Cartagena is on the northern coast of Colombia, on the Caribbean. It is one of the country's main beach resorts and, because of its history, is also one of the most interesting cities in South America. The old walled city of Cartagena, founded by Pedro de Heredia in 1533, was one of the storage centers for goods sent from Spain to its American colonies and for the treasures collected by the Spaniards in the colonies to be sent back to Spain. Cartagena is almost completely surrounded by water: the Caribbean, the Bay of Cartagena, and lakes and lagoons. This made it open to attacks by pirates, which is why walls and fortresses were constructed around the city for protection. Cartagena declared its independence from Spain on November 11, 1811.

II. Comparative Constructions

- In Spanish and in English the comparative construction is used to describe an object or person as having more, less, or the same amount of a characteristic as another. This construction is the comparison of *superiority, inferiority,* and *equality.*

- In Spanish, the comparison of superiority is formed by **más** + adjective + **que** *(more . . . than):*

El parque zoológico es *más moderno que* el acuario.	*The zoo is more modern than the aquarium.*

- The comparison of inferiority is formed by **menos** + adjective + **que** *(less . . . than):*

Diana es *menos ambiciosa que* Laura.	*Diana is less ambitious than Laura. (Diana is not as ambitious as Laura.)*

- The comparison of equality is formed by **tan** + adjective + **como** *(as . . . as):*

Mi hermano es *tan inteligente como* mi hermana.	*My brother is as intelligent as my sister.*

- Some adjectives have irregular comparative forms and do not use **más** or **menos** in expressing comparisons:

bueno *good*	**mejor** *better*
malo *bad*	**peor** *worse*
joven *young*	**menor** *younger*
viejo *old*	**mayor** older

La clase de historia es *mejor* que la clase de biología.	*History class is better than biology class.*
La carretera es *peor* que la avenida.	*The highway is worse than the avenue.*
—Tito es *mayor* que Ramón, ¿no?	*"Tito is older than Ramón, isn't he?"*
—Sí. Ramón es *menor* y más malo que su primo.	*"Yes. Ramón is younger and worse (more badly behaved) than his cousin."*

Note: Más bueno and **más malo** are used to refer to moral qualities.

■ To say that you like something better than something else, you use **más,** not **mejor:**

Me gusta *más* esta computadora.	*I like this computer better.*
Nos gustan *más* estos bocadillos.	*We like these sandwiches better.*

■ Adverbs are compared in the same way as adjectives:

Aurelia habla más/menos discretamente que Sergio.	*Aurelia speaks more/less tactfully than Sergio does.*
Aurelia habla tan discretamente como Sergio.	*Aurelia speaks as tactfully as Sergio does.*

■ In comparisons of equality with verbs and nouns, **tan** changes to **tanto.** **Tanto** does not change form with verbs; however, with nouns, **tanto** agrees with its noun in number and gender:

Nosotros leemos más/menos que Uds.	*We read more/less than you do.*
Nosotros leemos tanto como Uds.	*We read as much as you do.*
La torta tiene más/menos mantequilla que el pastel.	*The cake has more/less butter than the pie does.*
La torta tiene tanta mantequilla como el pastel.	*The cake has as much butter as the pie does.*
Nieves compró tantos vestidos como Dora.	*Nieves bought as many dresses as Dora.*

Notes:

1. **Que** *(than)* is followed by subject pronouns unless the pronoun is the direct object or indirect object of the verb. In that case, **que** is followed by **a** + pronoun:

Yo leo más que tú.	*I read more than you do.*
A mí me gusta leer más que a ti.	*I like to read more than you do.*

2. In comparisons with all other things or people, **que** is followed by **nada** and **nadie.** In English, *anything else* and *anyone else* are used:

Sol quiere ganar dinero más que nada.	*Sol wants to earn money more than anything else.*
Andrés juega fútbol mejor que nadie.	*Andrés plays soccer better than anyone else.*

3. **Que** is replaced by **de** before a numeral:

Tengo más de diez mil libros.   *I have more than 10,000 books.*

H. Vamos a comparar: adjetivos. Combine each pair of sentences into a single sentence expressing a comparison with **más**. Then write another sentence expressing a comparison with **menos**.

Modelo   Marga es amable. / Beti es más amable.
   ➤ Beti es más amable que Marga.
   ➤ Marga es menos amable que Beti.

1. La joyería es elegante. / La perfumería es más elegante.

   perfumería es más elegante que...
   joyería es menos elegante que

2. La sopa de gallina está sabrosa. / La sopa de legumbres está más sabrosa.

   Sopa legumbres está mas sabrosa que
   Sopa gallina está menos que sopa legumbres

3. El correo es útil. / El correo electrónico es más útil.

   electrónico es más útil que el correo
   el correo es menos útil que electrónico

4. La clínica está cerca. / El hospital está más cerca.

   hospital está mas cerca que clinica
   clinica está ee menos cerca que hospital

5. El hermano de Víctor es joven. / El hermano de Pilar es mayor.

   hermano de Pilar es mayor que Victor
   Victor es joven que Pilar

6. Las chaquetas de lana son caras. / Las chaquetas de cuero son más caras.

   de cuero son más caras que de lana
   de lana son menos caras que de cuero

7. Amparo y Concha son graciosas. / Teo y Julio son más graciosos.

   Teo y Julio son más graciosos que Amparo y Concha
   Amparo y Concha son menos graciosas que Teo y Julio

I. **Vamos a comparar: adverbios.** For each set of words, write three sentences to compare adverbs, using **más, menos,** and **tan.**

Modelo él / aprender las fechas rápidamente / ella
➤ Él aprende las fechas más rápidamente que ella.
➤ Ella aprende las fechas menos rápidamente que él.
➤ Él aprende las fechas tan rápidamente como ella.

1. nosotros / tomar apuntes cuidadosamente / ellos

   tomamos más cuidadosamente que ellos

   menos que

   tan como

2. Catarina / toca el violín artísticamente / Sofía

   _____

   _____

   _____

3. los estudiantes españoles / pronunciar inglés correctamente / los estudiantes franceses

   _____

   _____

   _____

4. Daniel / nadar bien / Miguel

   _____

   _____

   _____

J. **Igualdad.** Write sentences that express comparison of equality with adjectives.

Modelo su pintura / hermosa / su escultura
➤ Su pintura es tan hermosa como su escultura.

1. Sarita / traviesa / su hermana menor

   es tan traviesa que su

2. el collar de perlas / costoso / el anillo de oro

es tan costoso como el anillo

3. Pablo / impaciente / Rodrigo

es tan impaciente como

4. los hijos de los Alba / idealistas / sus padres

son tan idealistas como

5. Lidia / rara / Mariana

es tan rara como

6. la torre / alta / el rascacielos

es tan alta como

K. Comparaciones de igualdad. Write sentences that show comparison of equality of nouns. Remember that **tanto** agrees with its noun in number and gender.

Modelo Jorge / tomar / exámenes / Felisa
➤ Jorge toma tantos exámenes como Felisa.

1. Magdalena / ahorrar / dinero / su marido

ahorra tanto dinero como

2. yo / enviar / paquetes y tarjetas / Ud.

envío tantos paquetes y tarjetas como ud.

3. tú / comer / bombones / Gracielita

comes tantos bombones como Gracielita

4. el restaurante inglés / servir / carne / el restaurante italiano

sirve tanta carne como

5. nosotros / tener / tarjetas de crédito / Armando

tenemos tantas tarjetas de crédito como Armando

6. los ingenieros / saber / estadística / los contables

saben tanta estadística como los cantables

III. Superlative Constructions and the Absolute Superlative

■ There is no special superlative form in Spanish. In English the superlative is expressed with *most* or the suffix *-est*. To suggest a superlative in Spanish, the definite article (or possessive adjective) is used with the noun that the adjective modifies. Compare the following comparative and superlative sentences:

—**Quiero ver una maleta más grande.**   *"I want to see a larger suitcase."*

—**Aquí tiene Ud.** *la maleta más grande* **que vendemos.**   *"Here's the largest suitcase we sell."*

■ After a superlative, **de** is used to express *in*:

Este barrio es el más antiguo *de* la ciudad.   *This neighborhood is the oldest one in the city.*

■ The Spanish suffix **-ísimo**, called the *absolute superlative*, is added to adjectives to suggest the idea of *very*. Adjectives that end in **-ísimo** have four forms:

un libro muy interesante = **un libro interesantísimo**

unos libros muy interesantes = **unos libros interesantísimos**

una flor muy hermosa = **una flor hermosísima**

unas flores muy hermosas = **unas flores hermosísimas**

Note: To keep the sound of the original adjective, the spelling changes in some words when **-ísimo** is added: **c** changes to **qu**, **g** changes to **gu**, and **z** changes to **c**:

rico ➤ **riquísimo**   largo ➤ **larguísimo**   feliz ➤ **felicísimo**

L. Superlativos. Use the words given to form sentences that express the superlative of adjectives. (Don't forget to make the adjectives agree with their nouns.)

Modelo   Clara / alumna / diligente / clase
➤ Clara es la alumna más diligente de la clase.

1. Augusto Reyes / actor / talentoso / obra

_____

2. la capital / ciudad / moderno / país

_____

3. el banco nacional / edificio / alto / centro

_____

4. Alejandra y Simón / médicos / trabajador / hospital

_____

5. Felipe Gutiérrez / empleado / ambicioso / compañía

_____

6. Marta Ibáñez / profesora / conocido / colegio

_____

M. Un anuncio *(An ad)*. Rewrite the following newspaper ad about a youth hostel. Change each phrase with **muy** to the correct form of the adjective ending in **-ísimo.**

Modelo   El albergue juvenil es muy grande.
       ➤ El albergue juvenil es grandísimo.

Palabras útiles

el albergue juvenil *youth hostel*
los servicios *facilities, amenities*

---

1. Nuestros precios son muy bajos.

_____

2. Las habitaciones son muy hermosas.

_____

3. Nuestros servicios son muy buenos.

_____

4. Los empleados son muy simpáticos.

_____

5. Nuestra piscina es muy larga y muy ancha.

_____

6. Cada cliente está muy feliz.

_____

N. Preguntas personales. Answer the following questions in complete Spanish sentences. Use adverbs and constructions of comparison in your answers.

1. ¿Eres responsable / discreto(a) / honesto(a)? ¿Más o menos que tus amigos?

   _____

2. ¿Tienes hermanos mayores y menores? ¿Tus amigos tienen más o menos?

   _____

3. ¿Quién es más (menos) intelectual / idealista / realista / diligente / perezoso? ¿Tú o tus compañeros?

   _____

   _____

4. ¿Eres alto(a) / moreno(a) / rubio(a)? ¿Más o menos que tus padres y tus hermanos?

   _____

   _____

5. ¿Qué cosa es más/menos divertida o tan divertida como otra cosa? (las películas, los conciertos, las obras de teatro, la discoteca, los museos, el parque zoológico, el centro comercial)

   _____

   _____

   _____

O. Composición. Write a composition of eight to ten sentences in which you compare two cities, books, films, or restaurants. Study the examples for ideas:

Nueva York tiene más museos que mi ciudad.
Esta novela policíaca es menos interesante que esa novela histórica.
La película "Titánico" es tan divertida como la película "Lo que el viento se llevó" *(Gone with the Wind)*.
Como tan bien en el restaurante mexicano como en el restaurante chino.

Direct Object Pronouns; Indirect Object Pronouns;
***Gustar** and Other Verbs of This Pattern;*
Double Object Pronouns

I. Direct Object Pronouns

- Direct object pronouns can replace direct object nouns (that is, the people or things already mentioned). Study the chart of the direct object pronouns:

	singular	plural
first person	me	nos
second person	te	os
third person *(masc.)*	lo	los
third person *(fem.)*	la	las

- The pronouns **lo, la, los,** and **las** refer to both people and things. Direct object pronouns precede the conjugated verb in Spanish; they follow it in English:

No encuentro el diccionario.	*I can't find the dictionary.*
No *lo* encuentro.	*I can't find it.*
No encuentro al profesor.	*I can't find the teacher.*
No *lo* encuentro.	*I can't find him.*

- **Lo, la, los,** and **las** are also the direct object pronouns for **Ud.** and **Uds.** They mean *you,* as well as *him, her, it,* and *them:*

Lo busco, señor.	*I'm looking for you, Sir.*
Señorita, yo la llevo a la librería.	*Miss, I'll take you to the bookstore.*
No los comprendemos.	{ *We don't understand them.* { *We don't understand you.*

- The personal **a** labels a specific person as the direct object noun (see Chapter 7). A phrase made up of the personal **a** + a noun can be replaced by a single direct object pronoun:

—¿Conoces a Verónica Azorín?	*"Do you know Verónica Azorín?"*
—Sí, la conozco.	*"Yes, I know her."*

- In the verb + infinitive construction, the direct object pronoun may precede the first (conjugated) verb, or it can be attached to the infinitive:

—¿Quieres comprar estas camisetas?	*"Do you want to buy these T-shirts?"*
—Sí, *las* voy a comprar. }	*"Yes, I'm going to buy them."*
—Sí, voy a *comprarlas*. }	

- In the progressive tenses (see Chapter 5), the direct object pronoun can be placed before the conjugated form of **estar,** or it can be attached to the present participle. When the pronoun is attached to the present participle in writing, an accent mark is added to the vowel before the **-ndo:**

—¿Están ordenando su cuarto?	*"Are they straightening up their room?"*
—Sí, *lo* están ordenando. ⎫	
—Sí, están *ordenándolo.* ⎭	*"Yes, they're straightening it up."*

- In compound tenses, such as the present perfect tense (see Chapter 17), the direct object pronoun must be placed before the form of the auxiliary (helping) verb **haber:**

—¿Ya has abierto las cajas?	*"Have you opened the boxes already?"*
—No, no *las he abierto* todavía.	*"No, I haven't opened them yet."*

- With commands (see Chapter 15), the direct object pronoun is attached to affirmative command forms. An accent mark is added to the stressed vowel of the command form, except in the case of one-syllable commands. The direct object pronoun precedes the negative command forms:

—¿Por qué no llamas a Patricia?	*"Why don't you call Patricia?"*
—*Llámala* tú.	*"You call her."* (or *"Call her yourself."*)
—¿Hago la cena ahora?	*"Shall I make dinner now?"*
—Sí, por favor, *hazla.*	*"Yes, please, make it."*
—No, *no la hagas* todavía.	*"No, don't make it yet."*

A. **¡Qué banquete!** *(What a feast!)* When people are asked if they have, need, or are cooking certain ingredients for a sumptuous meal, they answer yes. Write their responses using the appropriate direct object pronouns.

Modelo —¿Tienes azúcar?
➤ —Sí, lo tengo.

La comida

la aceituna *olive*

el banquete *feast, banquet*

los camarones *shrimp*

---

1. —¿Tienes plátanos?

   — *Sí, los tengo*

2. —¿Beatriz necesita maíz?

   — *Sí, Beatriz la necesita*

3. —¿Tienen Uds. uvas y naranjas?

— Sí, ~~Een~~ las tenemos

4. —¿Guillermo y Nati cocinan camarones?

— Sí, los cocinan

5. —¿Prepara Ud. papas?

— Sí, las preparo

6. —¿Usamos aceite de oliva?

— Sí, ~~la~~ la usan

7. —¿Cocinas tomates?

— Sí, los cocino

8. —¿Necesitáis aceitunas?

— Sí, las necesitamos

Productos agrícolas (Agricultural products)

- Ecuador is the leading producer of bananas in the world. It also produces and exports coffee, cocoa, potatoes, and seafood, especially shrimp. Shrimp farming is currently an important economic activity for the country.
- Foods such as tomatoes, corn, and potatoes were indigenous to the New World and were unknown in Europe until the **conquistadores** brought them back to Spain in the sixteenth century. The potato originated in the highland region (**el altiplano**) of Peru and was the main food of the Incas. After the Spaniards conquered Peru in 1536, they began to use potatoes as cheap food for the sailors on the ships bound for Spain. Thus the potato became known in Europe. **Papa,** a word of Quechuan origin, is used throughout Spanish America; **patata** is used in Spain.
- Spain is an important producer and exporter of olives, olive oil, grapes, and citrus fruits.

B. Ud. y Uds. The direct object pronouns **lo** and **la** replace **Ud.,** and **los** and **las** replace **Uds.** Answer the following questions using these direct object pronouns in your answers.

Modelo —¿Me mira Ud.?

➤ —Sí, señora, <u>la miro</u> .

1. —¿Me comprende Ud.?

   —Sí, señor, <u>lo comprendo</u>

2. —¿Nos lleva Ud.?

   —Sí, señores, <u>lo llevo</u>

3. —¿Me espera Ud.?

   —Sí, señorita, <u>la espero</u>

4. —¿Me mira Ud.?

   —Sí, profesor, <u>lo miro</u>

5. —¿Me ve Ud.?

   —Sí, señor, <u>lo veo</u>

6. —¿Nos busca Ud.?

   —Sí, señoras, <u>la busco</u>

7. —¿Me ayuda Ud.?

   —Sí, señorita, <u>la ayudo</u>

8. —¿Nos conoce Ud.?

   —Sí, señores, <u>lo conozco</u>

C. **Vamos de compras.** You are going on a shopping trip with your friends. Answer the questions about the purchases using the verb + infinitive construction and direct object pronouns. Write each response in two ways: first place the direct object pronoun before the conjugated verb, and then attach it to the infinitive. (Write dashes for dialogue exchanges.)

Modelo —¿Compras zapatos? (ir a)
➤ —Sí, los voy a comprar. / —Sí, voy a comprarlos.

La ropa

los calcetines *socks (Spain)*

las mallas *tights*

las medias *socks (Spanish America); stockings (Spain)*

la ropa interior *underwear*

---

1. —¿Alicia compra ese abrigo marrón? (pensar)

   Sí, lo pensa comprar / Sí, pensa comprarlo

2. —¿Compran Uds. mallas? (querer)

   Sí, las ~~quier~~queremos comprar / Sí, queremos comprarlas

3. —¿Compro esta chaqueta de lana? (deber)

   Sí, la debe comprar / Sí, debe comprarla

4. —¿Roberto y Ricardo compran calcetines? (ir a)

   Sí, los van a comprar / Sí, van a comprarlos

5. —¿Compra Ud. el traje de baño? (tener que)

   Sí, lo tengo que comprar / Sí, tengo que comprarlo

6. —¿Eduardo compra pantalones? (poder)

   Sí, los puede comprar / Sí, puede comprarlos

7. —¿Gilda y yo compramos medias? (deber)

   Sí, las deben comprar / Sí deben comprarlas

8. —¿Compráis ropa interior? (pensar)

   Sí, la pensamos comprar / Sí pensamos comprarla

D. En la escuela nocturna *(At night school).* Confirm that people are taking certain classes at night school. Use the present progressive tense and direct object pronouns in your answers. Write each answer in two ways.

Modelo   Eva y Tomás / tomar / cerámica
➤ Eva y Tomás están tomándola. / Eva y Tomás la están tomando.

Las materias

las ciencias de medio ambiente *environmental sciences*

la contabilidad *accounting*

cursar *to take a course in*

los estudios de psicología *psychology workshops*

la planificación urbana *urban planning*

el seminario de hostelería *seminar in hotel management*

---

1. Paula / tomar / el seminario de hostelería

   está tomándolo / lo está tomando

2. yo / cursar / contabilidad

   estoy cursándola / la estoy cursando

3. tú / estudiar / ciencias de medio ambiente

   estás estudiándolas / las estás estudiand

4. nosotros / seguir / las clases de economía

   estamos siguiéndolas / las

5. Pamela y Federico / estudiar / planificación urbana

   están estudiándola

6. Ud. / tomar / los estudios de psicología

   está tomándolos

II. Indirect Object Pronouns

■ Indirect objects tell to whom something is given, said, or done, or for whom something is intended. They most commonly refer to people and, as nouns, they are preceded by the preposition **a**. Indirect object pronouns can replace the indirect object nouns and phrases. Study their forms in the chart:

	singular	plural
first person	me	nos
second person	te	os
third person	le	les

■ In Spanish, an indirect object noun is usually accompanied by the corresponding indirect object pronoun, **le** or **les**:

—¿*Les* das un regalo a tus tíos?	*"Are you giving your aunt and uncle a gift?"*
—Claro. Y *le* doy uno a mi prima también.	*"Of course. And I'm giving one to my cousin too."*

■ **Le** can mean *to him, to her,* or *to you* (**a Ud.**). **Les** can mean *to them* or *to you* (**a Uds.**). Often, it's necessary to clarify to whom **le** or **les** is referring. To do this, the phrase **a** + pronoun or **a** + noun can be added to the sentence:

Le pregunto.	*I ask him/her/you.*
Le pregunto *a él.*	*I ask him.*
Le pregunto *al agente de viajes.*	*I ask the travel agent.*

■ Indirect object pronouns follow the same rules of position as direct object pronouns. They either precede a conjugated verb or are attached to an infinitive:

Me traen un recuerdo.	*They're bringing me a souvenir.*
Me van a traer un recuerdo.	*They are going to bring me a*
Van a *traerme* un recuerdo.	*souvenir.*

■ Indirect object pronouns precede **estar** or are attached to the present participle in the progressive tenses (see Chapter 5):

Les estamos mostrando el álbum.	
Estamos *mostrándoles* el álbum.	*We're showing them the album.*

■ Indirect object pronouns precede the auxiliary verb **haber** in compound tenses (see Chapter 17):

¿*Te han* explicado el problema?	*Have they explained the problem to you?*

■ Indirect object pronouns are attached to affirmative command forms (see Chapter 15). An accent mark is added to the stressed vowel of the command form, except in the case of one-syllable commands:

Dígame la fecha.	*Tell me the date.*
Dime la dirección.	*Tell me the address.*

- Some common verbs that take an indirect object of the person (**le... a alguien**) and a direct object that is a thing (**algo**):

   contarle algo a alguien *to tell something to someone*

   darle algo a alguien *to give something to someone*

   decirle algo a alguien *to say, to tell something to someone*

   devolverle algo a alguien *to return something to someone*

   enseñarle algo a alguien *to teach, show something to someone*

   entregarle algo a alguien *to hand over something to someone*

   enviarle algo a alguien *to send something to someone*

   escribirle algo a alguien *to write something to someone*

   explicarle algo a alguien *to explain something to someone*

   mandarle algo a alguien *to send something to someone*

   mostrarle algo a alguien *to show something to someone*

   ofrecerle algo a alguien *to offer something to someone*

   pedirle algo a alguien *to ask someone for something*

   recordarle algo a alguien *to remind someone of something*

   regalarle algo a alguien *to give something to someone as a gift*

   traerle algo a alguien *to bring something to someone*

- With some verbs the indirect object indicates from whom something is done or acquired:

   comprarle algo a alguien *to buy something from someone*

   exigirle algo a alguien *to demand something from/of someone*

   ganarle algo a alguien *to win something from someone*

   robarle algo a alguien *to steal something from someone*

E. ¿A quién(es)? Rewrite the following sentences. Change the indirect object pronoun based on the cue in parentheses.

Modelo Les escribo una tarjeta. (a ella) ➤ Le escribo una tarjeta.

1. Te doy el cheque mañana. (a Uds.)

   Les doy el cheque mañana

2. Os vamos a ofrecer una limonada. (a él)

   Le vamos a ofrecer una limonada

3. Quieren enseñarle el jardín. (a nosotros)

   Nos quieren enseñar el jardín

4. Les devuelve el paraguas. (a ti)

Te devuelve el paraguas

5. Te envían unos paquetes. (a mí)

Me envían unos paquetes

6. ¿Nos dicen la verdad? (a Ud.)

Le dicen la verdad

7. Me cuentan la historia. (a vosotros)

Os cuentan la historia

8. Deben recordarnos la fecha. (a ella)

Le deben recordar la fecha

F. **Una boda.** Tell about the wedding you are attending. Write sentences with the words given, and add the correct indirect object pronoun to each sentence.

Modelo   los padres de Teresa / hacer / una boda magnífica / a su hija
➤ Los padres de Teresa le hacen una boda magnífica a su hija.

La boda

echar un brindis *to toast*   **el pastelero** *pastry chef*

el invitado *guest*   **el pastor** *minister*

la modista *dressmaker*   **el ramo de flores** *bouquet*

los novios *bride and groom; newlyweds*   **tirar** *to throw*

---

1. los invitados / dar / muchos regalos de boda / a los novios

les dan

2. la modista / hacer / el traje de novia / a Teresa

Le hace

3. el pastelero / mostrar / el pastel de boda / a la pareja

Le muestra

4. Juan Carlos / entregar / el anillo de boda / a su novia

Le entrega

➤➤➤➤➤

5. los novios / contestar / que sí / al pastor

   le contestan

6. Teresa / tirar / su ramo de flores / a sus amigas

   les tira

7. nosotros / echar / un brindis / a los novios

   les echamos

8. Teresa y Juan Carlos / dar / besos y abrazos / a nosotros

   nos dan

III. *Gustar* and Other Verbs of This Pattern

■ Certain Spanish verbs are almost always used with an indirect object pronoun. The most common verb of this type is **gustar** *(to like)*. **Gustar** agrees with the subject of the sentence, which follows the verb. (Note that this construction is different from the English equivalent of **gustar.**)

Me gusta el cuadro.	*I like the picture.*
Me gustan los carteles.	*I like the posters.*

■ Some verbs that follow the same pattern as **gustar:**

dolerle (o ➤ ue) a alguien *to hurt, to ache*

encantarle a alguien *to love something*

faltarle a alguien *to be missing something, not to have something, to be short of*

hacerle falta a alguien *to need something*

importarle a alguien *to care about something, to mind*

interesarle a alguien *to be interested in something*

parecerle a alguien *to think of; to seem*

quedarle a alguien *to have something left*

tocarle a alguien *to be someone's turn*

Notes:

1. In the phrase **hacerle falta**, **falta** is a noun and doesn't change:

Me hace falta un bolígrafo.	*I need a pen.*
Me hacen falta unos bolígrafos.	*I need some pens.*

2. A phrase of **a** + noun or **a** + pronoun is placed (usually) before **le** and **les** to clarify or emphasize the indirect object pronouns:

A Marcos le faltan diez dólares.	*Marcos is short ten dollars.*
A él le faltan diez dólares.	*He's short ten dollars.*

- When the subject of **gustar** (and verbs like **gustar**) is an infinitive, the verb is always in the third-person singular:

  —¿Qué te gusta hacer los sábados?   *"What do you like to do on Saturdays?"*

  —Me gusta montar en bicicleta o jugar al tenis.   *"I like to go bike riding or play tennis."*

G. Me interesan... Tell the things that people like, love, are interested in, or need. Change the subject of each sentence to the plural and make all necessary changes.

Modelo   A mis amigos les gusta el programa.
        ➤ A mis amigos les gustan los programas.

1. A Teo y a mí nos queda un examen.

   _____

2. Me encanta esa película.

   _____

3. A Ud. le encanta esta videocinta.

   _____

4. Te hace falta un cuaderno.

   _____

5. A nuestros padres les importa nuestra idea.

   _____

6. A Magda le parece interesante la materia.

   _____

7. A Ricardo le duele el brazo.

   _____

8. Os interesa el deporte.

   _____

IV. Double Object Pronouns

- In conversation, as well as in writing, both an indirect object pronoun and a direct object pronoun are often used in the same sentence. When there is a single conjugated verb, they are placed before the verb. The indirect object pronoun always comes before the direct object pronoun:

  —**Quiero ver tu calculadora.**   *"I want to see your calculator.*
    ¿Me la **enseñas?**   *Will you show it to me?"*
  —**Claro.** *Te la* **enseño ahora mismo.**   *"Of course. I'll show it to you right now."*

- When a third-person indirect object pronoun (**le** or **les**) precedes a third-person direct object pronoun (**lo, la, los,** or **las**), the indirect object pronoun changes to **se:**

  le / les + lo ➤ **se lo**
  le / les + la ➤ **se la**
  le / les + los ➤ **se los**
  le / les + las ➤ **se las**

  —**¿El profesor les explica la**   *"Does the teacher explain grammar*
    gramática?   *to them?"*
  —**Sí,** *se la* **explica bien.**   *"Yes, he explains it to them well."*

  —**¿Ud. le da el informe?**   *"Are you giving him the report?"*
  —**Sí,** *se lo* **doy.**   *"Yes, I'm giving it to him."*

- When indirect and direct object pronouns are added to an infinitive, a present participle, or an affirmative command, an accent mark must be added, even in the case of one-syllable infinitives and command forms. Double object pronouns cannot be separated from each other:

  Voy a hacerle el desayuno. = **Voy a hacérselo. / Se lo voy a hacer.**
  Están sirviéndonos la cena. = **Están sirviéndonosla. / Nos la están sirviendo.**
  Dime la verdad. = **Dímela.**

- Sentences with **se** (substituting for **le** or **les**) can be ambiguous. To clarify to whom **se** refers, a phrase with **a** + prepositional pronoun is added:

  Se las escribo *a él.*   *I write them to him.*
  Se lo decimos *a ella.*   *We're telling it to her.*

H. Oraciones con dos complementos *(Sentences with double object pronouns).*
Rewrite each sentence by changing the direct object noun to a pronoun and making all the necessary changes.

Modelo   Te doy el libro de texto después. ➤ Te lo doy después.

1. Me mandan los paquetes.   _____

2. ¿Le regalas estas flores?   _____

3. Les preparamos el almuerzo.   _____

4. Os traigo la ropa.   _____

5. Te devuelve el impermeable. _____

6. Nos entrega los documentos. _____

7. ¿No les cuentas la idea? _____

8. Me muestran las fotos, ¿no? _____

I. **¿Quién y cuándo?** Tell who is doing what or when they are doing it. Answer the questions with double object pronouns and the cues. Write each answer in two ways. (Don't forget to add dashes for dialogue exchanges.)

Modelo —¿Quién te va a prestar la calculadora? (Pati)
➤ —Pati va a prestármela. / —Pati me la va a prestar.

1. —¿Quién está enseñándole el jardín a Lorenzo? (Sofía)

   _____

2. —¿Cuándo van Uds. a hacerles los sándwiches a los niños? (en un rato)

   _____

3. —¿Quién te quiere comprar la pulsera? (Nicanor)

   _____

4. —¿Cuándo piensa Ud. mandarles las tarjetas? (la semana próxima)

   _____

5. —¿Quiénes pueden contarle a Ud. la historia? (Sergio y Beti)

   _____

6. —¿Cuándo tienes que entregarle el ensayo a la profesora? (lo antes posible)

   _____

7. —¿Quién está poniéndole los zapatos a Joselito? (su mamá)

   _____

8. —¿Cuándo debemos mostrarles el módem a los amigos? (el jueves)

   _____

J. Preguntas personales. Answer the following questions in complete Spanish sentences.

1. ¿Qué asignatura *(school subject)* te interesa más? ¿Por qué?

   _____

2. ¿Qué te gusta hacer durante las vacaciones? ¿Qué te interesa ver?

   _____

3. ¿Qué te parece la vida cultural de tu ciudad (pueblo)?

   _____

4. ¿Qué te importa más que nada en la vida?

   _____

5. A tus amigos y a ti, ¿qué les encanta hacer los fines de semana?

   _____

K. Composición. Write a composition of eight to ten sentences describing the things you and your family like to do. Use the verbs **gustar, encantar, interesar, parecer,** and others, as well as direct and indirect object pronouns.

CHAPTER 12

Prepositions; Prepositional Pronouns

I. Prepositions

In Spanish, as in English, a preposition is a function word that joins two or more words and shows a relationship between them.

A

■ The preposition **a** is used with verbs of motion. It shows motion toward a place:

—¿Adónde van Uds.?	*"Where are you going?"*
—Vamos al teatro.	*"We're going to the theater."*

■ **A** is used to connect verbs of motion to an infinitive to express purpose:

Felipe y Norma vienen a vernos.	*Felipe and Norma are coming to see us.*

■ **A** is used to link a verb with a specific, animate direct object. In this function, it is called the personal **a** (see Chapter 7):

Busco a Carolina pero no la encuentro.	*I'm looking for Carolina, but I can't find her.*

■ **A** is used with an indirect object pronoun:

—¿A quién le regalas esos libros?	*"To whom are you giving those books?"*
—Se los regalo a Pedro.	*"I'm giving them to Pedro."*

■ **A** can be the equivalent of *at* or *on* in certain expressions of location and time:

—¿Queda la librería aquí a la derecha?	*"Is the bookstore here on the right?"*
—No, queda al final de la calle.	*"No, it's at the end of the street."*
—¿A qué hora abre?	*"At what time does it open?"*
—A las nueve de la mañana.	*"At 9 A.M."*

■ In certain expressions, **a** is used to indicate how something is done:

Preparan platos a la española.	*They prepare Spanish-style dishes.*

■ **A** is used in certain idioms and expressions:

a menudo *often*	**a veces** *sometimes*
a sus órdenes *at your service*	**al aire libre** *open-air*
a tres millas de la casa *three miles from the house*	**una vez al año** *once a year*

A. **¿*A* o nada?** Complete each of the following sentences by adding the preposition **a** where necessary. If no preposition is needed, mark the blank with an *X*. (Remember to use the contraction **al.**)

1. Piensan ir _____ la embajada el viernes.

2. Son _____ las cuatro menos cuarto.

3. Le estoy escribiendo una carta _____ mi hermano.

4. Gerardo hace un viaje de negocios dos veces _____ mes.

5. Van a llegar _____ el rancho _____ caballo.

6. Preferimos conocer _____ Bilbao en octubre.

7. Elisa regresa _____ la residencia _____ medianoche.

8. ¿_____ cuántos kilómetros de San Sebastián vives?

9. Los Bermúdez deben _____ salir _____ cenar _____ las ocho.

10. ¡Tienes que probar el pollo _____ la madrileña!

En el norte de España

- **Bilbao** (*Bilbo* in Basque) is the capital of the Basque province of Vizcaya, near the north coast of Spain. On the Nervión River, it is Spain's historical hub of the vast iron, steel, chemical, and shipbuilding industries. Bilbao is attempting to change its image as a dreary industrial city in hopes of attracting visitors. The vital tourism industry that bolsters Spain's economy does not extend to Bilbao. As part of its attempt at economic and urban renewal, Bilbao became the home of the $100 million Guggenheim Museum in October 1997. Designed by the American architect Frank Gehry, it sits on the banks of the Nervión, attracting attention because of its unusual titanium-plated forms that jut out in surprising directions. The Basque terrorist group E.T.A. had planned to disrupt the inauguration of the Guggenheim by King Juan Carlos. The terrorists had killed a Basque police officer days before, and the city was in mourning. The new museum is seen by many as a symbol of the Basque people's rejection of separatist violence, a political as well as a cultural statement.
- Bilbao's other attractions include the **Museo de Bellas Artes;** the **Museo Arqueológico, Etnográfico e Histórico Vasco;** and the **Teatro Arriaga,** the nineteenth-century theater patterned after the Paris Opera. The local soccer team, **el Club Atlético de Bilbao,** is one of Spain's best teams. It plays at the **Estadio San Mamés.**
- **San Sebastián** (*Donostia* in Basque) is on the northern coast of Spain, on the Bay of Vizcaya in the Cantabrian Sea (**Mar Cantábrico**). It is the capital of the Basque province of Guipúzcoa, a tourist paradise that has the very opposite image of Bilbao. A splendid summer resort since the nineteenth century, it has beautiful scenery, beaches, jazz festivals, regattas, an international film festival, and regional Basque celebrations.

De

- The preposition **de** means *from:*

  —¿**De dónde vienes?**   *"Where are you coming from?"*
  —**Vengo de la biblioteca.**   *"I'm coming from the library."*

- **De** also shows origin, possession, what something is made of, and the contents of a container:

Somos de la Florida.	*We're from Florida. (origin)*
La mochila es de Marcia.	*The backpack is Marcia's. (possession)*
Mi suéter es de algodón.	*My sweater is cotton. (what something is made of)*
¡Qué caja de bombones!	*What a box of chocolates! (contents of a container)*

- **De** is used to express phrases that are equivalent to noun + noun (or gerund + noun) constructions in English:

Estamos en la parada de autobús.	*We're at the bus stop. (noun + noun)*
¿No te gusta el traje de baño?	*Don't you like the bathing suit? (gerund + noun)*

- **De** is equivalent to *about,* for example, when talking about a topic:

Siempre hablas de música.	*You always talk about music.*

- **De** is used in certain idiomatic expressions:

de cuadros *checkered*	**de rayas** *striped*
de ida y vuelta *round-trip*	**ir de compras** *to go shopping*

B. ¿*De o nada?* Complete each of the following sentences by adding the preposition **de** where it is needed. If no preposition is needed, mark the blank with an *X*. (Remember to use the contraction **del**.)

1. ¿_____ dónde son _____ vuestros abuelos?

2. Escucho discos _____ compactos _____ música clásica.

3. Carmen Rosa busca su libro _____ texto.

4. Los Ojeda están _____ viaje todo el mes.

5. Ellos no quieren jugar al fútbol _____ americano con nosotros.

6. Estos cinturones son _____ cuero.

7. Este suéter es _____ Diego.

8. Muy pronto vamos a salir _____ parque _____ atracciones.

C. En español, por favor. Express the following phrases in Spanish.

1. a cheese sandwich _____

2. some businessmen _____

3. the tennis court _____

4. a round-trip ticket _____

5. the bathing suits _____

6. a music store _____

7. adventure novels _____

8. the art museum _____

En

■ The preposition **en** shows location. Its English equivalents are *at*, *in*, and *on*:

—¿Está Jaime **en** el consultorio médico?	*"Is Jaime at the doctor's office?"*
—No, ya está **en** casa.	*"No, he's at home already."*
—¿Dónde están las fotos?	*"Where are the photos?"*
—Están **en** la mesa grande **en** la sala.	*"They're on the big table in the living room."*

■ **En** shows a period of time:

—Acabo de correr una milla **en** diez minutos.	*"I just ran a mile in ten minutes."*
—¡Y yo **en** veinte minutos!	*"And I, in twenty minutes!"*

■ **En** shows the means of transportation:

—¿Cómo viajan Uds. a México?	*"How are you traveling to Mexico?"*
—Vamos **en** tren.	*"We're going by train."*

■ **En** is used in certain idiomatic expressions:

en casa *at home*	**en seguida** *immediately*
en este momento *at this moment*	**estar en oferta** *to be on sale*
en otra oportunidad *at some other time*	

D. ***¿En* o nada?** Complete each of the following sentences by adding the preposition **en** where necessary. If no preposition is needed, mark the blank with an *X*.

1. Hay mucha sal _____ la sopa.

2. Regreso _____ quince minutos.

3. No pienso visitar a mis abuelos _____ el sábado.

4. Es imposible. El presidente no puede salir _____ este momento.

5. Los Pérez van _____ tren y vuelven _____ avión.

6. ¿Prefieres montar _____ bicicleta?

E. En español, por favor. Express the following sentences in Spanish.

1. We like to go by boat.

   _____

2. Paco is at the mall.

   _____

3. Pili is leaving in two hours.

   _____

4. We'll have lunch at some other time.

   _____

5. There are papers on the desk.

   _____

6. They rent *(alquilar)* an apartment in this building.

   _____

Con

■ The preposition **con** means *with:*

   —**¿Tomas algo con nosotros?**   *"Will you have something to drink with us?"*
   —**Claro. Tomo un té con limón.**   *"Of course. I'll have tea with lemon."*

■ **Con** links a container with its contents:

   una maleta con ropa vieja *a suitcase of old clothing*

   una bolsa con cerezas *a bag of cherries*

   un vaso con agua *a glass of water*

F. En español. Express the following phrases in Spanish.

1. Can you *(tú)* go with Iris?

   _____

2. We're drinking coffee with milk.

   _____

3. They always serve rice with the fish.

   _____

4. Are you *(Uds.)* coming with your children?

   _____

5. Nélida is bringing a bag of cookies.

   _____

6. I'm having lunch with my friends.

   _____

G. Las preposiciones. Complete the following sentences by writing the missing preposition(s). Use **a, de, en,** or **con.**

1. Venden cereal _____ una bolsa _____ papel.

2. Ramón siempre pide una hamburguesa _____ queso.

3. No encuentro mis llaves _____ esta mesa.

4. La tienda _____ ropa está _____ la izquierda.

5. ¿Por qué no llevas _____ los niños _____ circo?

6. Lupe juega _____ tenis _____ su hermano.

7. No voy a comprar el saco _____ rayas porque no hace juego _____ el

   pantalón _____ cuadros.

Compound prepositions

■ Some prepositions, called *compound prepositions*, are made up of two or more words:

al lado de *next to*	**después de** *after*
antes de *before*	**detrás de** *behind*
cerca de *near; about (approximately)*	**encima de** *on, upon, on top of*
debajo de *under, beneath*	**frente a** *across from, facing*
delante de *in front of*	**lejos de** *far from*

H. **¿Dónde y cuándo?** Complete the following sentences by writing in the missing compound prepositions. Use the contractions **del** or **al** where necessary.

1. Hay un jardín _____ *(behind)* el garaje.

2. Los niños deben regresar _____ *(before)* las seis y media.

3. Su casa no está _____ *(far from)* el museo.

4. Los zapatos están _____ *(under)* la cama.

5. La panadería está _____ *(next to)* la carnicería.

6. La heladería está _____ *(across from)* el cine.

7. Voy a la cafetería _____ *(after)* la clase de biología.

8. El televisor está _____ *(on top of)* el escritorio.

The prepositions *para* and *por*
Para

■ The preposition **para** usually means *for*. It shows destination:

Salimos para la escuela ahora.   *We're leaving for school now.*

■ **Para** is used to express the time by which something will be done:

Termino el informe para el viernes.   *I'll finish the report by Friday.*

■ **Para** is used to show purpose (often followed by an infinitive):

Practico el tenis todos los días   *I practice tennis every day in order*
   para jugar bien.   *to play well.*

■ **Para** indicates the person for whom something is done:

Estos regalos son para Joseli.   *These gifts are for Joseli.*

- **Para** indicates someone's opinion:

Para Beti, la película es maravillosa.   *In Beti's opinion, the movie is wonderful.*

Por

- The preposition **por,** meaning *for,* indicates how long something lasts (duration):

Van a estar de vacaciones por una semana.   *They'll be on vacation for a week.*

- **Por** expresses the means by which something is done:

Las amigas hablan por teléfono.   *The girlfriends are talking on the telephone.*

- **Por** is used to mean *through:*

Puedes salir por esta puerta.   *You can leave through this door.*

- **Por** also shows imprecise location, like the English preposition *around:*

Hay una farmacia por aquí, ¿no?   *There's a drugstore around here, isn't there?*

- **Por** expresses *for* in the sense of *in exchange for:*

Mis tíos pagan mucho dinero por su apartamento.   *My aunt and uncle pay a lot of money for their apartment.*

- Common expressions with **por:**

por ejemplo *for example*	**por la playa** *along the beach*
por eso *therefore, that's why*	**por la tarde** *in the afternoon*
por favor *please*	**por primera vez** *for the first time*
por fin *finally, at last*	**por supuesto** *of course*
por la mañana *in the morning*	**por todas partes** *everywhere*
por la noche *at night*	

Para vs. por

- Since both **para** and **por** mean *for,* the context of the sentence determines which one should be used:

Trabajo *para* la señora Ruiz.   *I'm working for Mrs. Ruiz. (she's the boss)*

Trabajo *por* la señora Ruiz.   *I'm working for Mrs. Ruiz. (in her place)*

I. *¿Para o por?* Complete the following dialogues by writing either **para** or **por** in the blanks.

1. —¿Cuándo sale el avión _para_ San Diego?

2. —Sale mañana _por_ la mañana.

3. —¿_para_ quién es este anillo? ¿Es _para_ tu mamá?

4. —¿_para_ ella? No creo. ¡Es _para_ mi novia!

5. —Lorenzo está hablando _por_ teléfono, ¿no?

6. —No, está mandando un mensaje _por_ correo electrónico.

7. —Alba, _por_ favor, ¿puedes pasar la aspiradora?

8. —_Por_ supuesto, Carmen. ¿Está la aspiradora _por_ aquí?

9. —¿Trabajas _para_ la señorita Durán en su oficina?

10. —Sí. Y esta semana trabajo _por_ ella porque está de viaje.

11. —¿_por_ qué ahorran Uds. dinero?

12. —_para_ viajar a España.

II. Prepositional Pronouns

■ After the prepositions **a, de, en, para,** and **por,** the subject pronouns are used, except for **yo** and **tú:**

para **mí**	para nosotros / nosotras
para **ti**	para vosotros / vosotras
para él	para ellos
para ella	para ellas
para Ud.	para Uds.

—¿Para quién es esta tarjeta?   *"Whom is this card for? For him or*
¿Para él o para ella?   *for her?"*
—¿No sabes? ¡Es para ti!   *"Don't you know? It's for you!"*

■ With the preposition **con,** the **yo** and **tú** forms are irregular: **conmigo** and **contigo:**

—¿Vas al dentista conmigo?   *"Are you going to the dentist with*
                                    me?"

—¿Al dentista? ¡No! ¡Voy contigo   *"To the dentist? No! I'll go with you*
al cine!   *to the movies!"*

J. Pronombres con preposiciones. Fill in the correct form of the prepositional pronouns based on the cues in parentheses.

1. a _____ (yo)   5. de _____ (ella)

2. para _____ (Uds.)   6. por _____ (nosotros)

3. con _____ (tú)   7. con _____ (yo)

4. por _____ (tú)   8. en _____ (él)

K. Preguntas personales. Answer the following questions in complete Spanish sentences.

1. ¿Para qué estudias español / historia / biología / álgebra?

_____

2. ¿Adónde vas después de esta clase? ¿De dónde vienes antes de esta clase?

_____

3. ¿Dónde queda tu casa / la biblioteca / el centro comercial / el supermercado? (*Use compound prepositions.*)

_____

4. ¿Qué cosas están en oferta ahora? ¿Qué piensas comprar?

_____

5. ¿A qué hora sales para tus clases / regresas a casa?

_____

6. ¿Dónde trabajas? ¿Para quién(es) trabajas? ¿Con quién(es) trabajas?

_____

_____

L. Composición. Write eight to ten sentences about your favorite place. Tell what it looks like by describing the location of certain things in relation to other things. Use compound prepositions in some of your sentences.

The Preterit Tense; *Hace* + Expression of Time + *que* + Verb in the Preterit

I. The Preterit Tense

Regular verbs in the preterit tense

■ The preterit tense is used to express events that were completed in the past. It is formed by adding the preterit-tense endings to the stem of regular **-ar, -er,** and **-ir** verbs:

TRABAJAR *TO WORK*

yo trabaj**é**	nosotros/nosotras trabaj**amos**
tú trabaj**aste**	vosotros/vosotras trabaj**asteis**
él ella } trabaj**ó** Ud.	ellos ellas } trabaj**aron** Uds.

COMER *TO EAT*

yo com**í**	nosotros/nosotras com**imos**
tú com**iste**	vosotros/vosotras com**isteis**
él ella } com**ió** Ud.	ellos ellas } com**ieron** Uds.

ESCRIBIR *TO WRITE*

yo escrib**í**	nosotros/nosotras escrib**imos**
tú escrib**iste**	vosotros/vosotras escrib**isteis**
él ella } escrib**ió** Ud.	ellos ellas } escrib**ieron** Uds.

Stem-changing verbs in the preterit

■ Stem-changing **-ar** and **-er** verbs (**e** ≻ **ie** and **o** ≻ **ue**) do not have changes in the vowel of the stem in any of the preterit-tense forms: *pensar:* **pensé, pensaste, pensó, pensamos, pensasteis, pensaron;** *volver:* **volví, volviste, volvió, volvimos, volvisteis, volvieron.**

■ Stem-changing **-ir** verbs do have a stem change in the preterit tense. The vowel in the stem changes from **e** to **i** or from **o** to **u** in the third-person singular and third-person plural forms:

PEDIR *TO ASK FOR*

yo pedí	nosotros/nosotras pedimos
tú pediste	vosotros/vosotras pedisteis
él ella } pidió Ud.	ellos ellas } pidieron Uds.

DORMIR *TO SLEEP*

yo dormí	nosotros/nosotras dormimos
tú dormiste	vosotros/vosotras dormisteis
él ⎫	ellos ⎫
ella ⎬ durmió	ellas ⎬ durmieron
Ud. ⎭	Uds. ⎭

Verbs with spelling changes in the preterit

■ Spanish verbs that end in **-car, -gar,** and **-zar** have spelling changes in the **yo** form of the preterit tense. There are no spelling changes in the other forms of the verb:

Verbs ending in **-car** change **c** to **qu** before adding **é: buscar** ➢ **busqué**

Verbs ending in **-gar** change **g** to **gu** before adding **é: llegar** ➢ **llegué**

Verbs ending in **-zar** change **z** to **c** before adding **é: comenzar** ➢ **comencé**

Note: Some verbs that have stem changes in the present tense do not have stem changes in the preterit. Among those verbs, however, are some that have spelling changes in the preterit:

jugar ➢ **jugué**	colgar ➢ **colgué**
empezar ➢ **empecé**	almorzar ➢ **almorcé**

■ Some **-er** and **-ir** verbs, such as **leer** and **oír,** have a vowel immediately preceding the preterit ending. They change **-ió** to **-yó** in the third-person singular form and **-ieron** to **-yeron** in the third-person plural form in the preterit. These verbs also have a written accent over the **i** of the **tú, nosotros,** and **vosotros** endings:

LEER *TO READ*

yo leí	nosotros/nosotras leímos
tú leíste	vosotros/vosotras leísteis
él ⎫	ellos ⎫
ella ⎬ leyó	ellas ⎬ leyeron
Ud. ⎭	Uds. ⎭

OÍR *TO HEAR*

yo oí	nosotros/nosotras oímos
tú oíste	vosotros/vosotras oísteis
él ⎫	ellos ⎫
ella ⎬ oyó	ellas ⎬ oyeron
Ud. ⎭	Uds. ⎭

Note: The verbs **creer** *(to think; to believe)* and **caer** *(to fall)* are conjugated like **leer** and **oír** in the preterit tense.

A. La sobremesa *(After-dinner chat)*. You and your family are finishing dinner and telling about your day. Form sentences with the words given, and write the verbs in the preterit tense.

Modelo   Roberto / tomar tres exámenes ➢ Roberto tomó tres exámenes.

1. yo / usar la computadora

   Yo usé la computadora

2. Uds. / nadar en la piscina

   Uds. nadaron en la piscina

3. Elena / alquilar una película

   Elena alquiló una película

4. tú / correr cuatro millas

   Tú corriste cuatro millas

5. nosotros / comprar útiles escolares

   Nosotros compramos útiles escolares

6. Ud. / asistir a un concierto

   Ud. asistieron un concierto

7. Ricardo y Virginia / caminar

   Ricardo y Virginia caminaron

8. vosotros / trabajar en la tienda

   Vosotros trabajasteis en la tienda

B. ¡Buen provecho! *(Enjoy your meal!)* Complete the following paragraph about a meal in a Madrid restaurant. Write the preterit form of each of the verbs in parentheses.

Juan, Laura y yo _salimos_ (1. salir) al restaurante Buen Provecho ayer. Juan y Laura _pidieron_ (2. pedir) gazpacho y merluza a la española. Yo _preferí_ (3. preferir) el escalope y la ensaladilla rusa. Nosotros _bebimos_ (4. beber) agua mineral con gas. De postre todos nosotros _comimos_ (5. comer) el dulce de membrillo con queso. Nos _encantó_ (6. encantar) la comida y la moza nos _sirvió_ (7. servir) muy bien. Juan nos _invitó_ (8. invitar) y _pagó_ (9. pagar) la cuenta. Y Laura y yo _dejamos_ (10. dejar) una buena propina.

¡A comer!

El **gazpacho** (cold soup made with tomatoes and other ingredients), **la merluza** (cod or hake), **el escalope** (boneless veal cutlet), **la ensaladilla rusa** (potato salad), and **el dulce de membrillo** (molded quince preserve, served with cheese for dessert) are commonly found on Spanish menus. Spaniards drink bottled water in restaurants as well as at home, selecting either **agua con gas** (carbonated water) or **agua sin gas** (noncarbonated water).

C. ¿Cuándo pasó? Tell when the following things happened by rewriting each sentence. Change the verb from the present to the preterit tense and add the cue in parentheses.

Modelo   Uds. venden su carro. (el año pasado)
➤ Uds. vendieron su carro el año pasado.

1. Ud. lee los anuncios en el periódico. (ayer)

   Ud. leyó las anuncios en el periódico ayer

2. María y Ud. miran una telenovela. (anoche)

   María y Ud. miraron una telenovela anoche

3. Compramos una videocasetera. (la semana pasada)

   Compramos una videocasetera la semana pasada

4. El tío Armando duerme la siesta. (esta tarde)

   El tío Armando durmió la siesta esta tarde

5. Yo oigo las noticias en la radio. (esta mañana)

   Yo oí las noticias en la radio esta mañana

6. Pedro cae enfermo. (el martes)

   Pedro cayó enfermo el martes

7. Sirves el desayuno. (a las ocho)

   Sirviste el desayuno a las ocho

8. Manejáis al campo. (anteayer)

   Manejásteis al campo anteayer

D. Ya lo hice. *(I already did it.)* Answer the following questions by saying that the things asked about were already done. Write verbs in the preterit tense, and change direct object nouns to pronouns in your answers. (Be sure to make the necessary spelling changes in the verbs.)

Modelo   —¿Cuándo vas a explicar tus ideas?
     ➤ —Ya las expliqué.

1. —¿Cuándo vas a almorzar?

   — Ya, almorcé

2. —¿Cuándo vas a comenzar el informe?

   — Ya, lo comencé

3. —¿Cuándo vas a navegar en el web?

   — Ya, lo navegué

4. —¿Cuándo vas a sacar al perro?

   — Ya, lo saqué

5. —¿Cuándo vas a jugar al fútbol?

   — Ya, lo jugué

6. —¿Cuándo vas a colocar la alfombra en la sala?

   — Ya, la coloqué

7. —¿Cuándo vas a colgar los carteles?

   — Ya, las colgué

8. —¿Cuándo vas a buscar las llaves?

   — Ya, las busqué

Irregular verbs in the preterit tense

■ There are several Spanish verbs that have irregular forms in the preterit tense. Most of these verbs have an irregular stem and use the following endings: **-e, -iste, -o, -imos, -isteis, -ieron** or **-eron.** Study the charts of the following irregular verbs:

DECIR *TO SAY; TO TELL*		**ESTAR** *TO BE*	
dije	dijimos	estuve	estuvimos
dijiste	dijisteis	estuviste	estuvisteis
dijo	dijeron	estuvo	estuvieron

HACER TO DO; TO MAKE

hice	hicimos
hiciste	hicisteis
hizo	hicieron

PODER CAN, TO BE ABLE

pude	pudimos
pudiste	pudisteis
pudo	pudieron

PONER TO PUT

puse	pusimos
pusiste	pusisteis
puso	pusieron

QUERER TO WANT; TO LOVE

quise	quisimos
quisiste	quisisteis
quiso	quisieron

SABER TO KNOW

supe	supimos
supiste	supisteis
supo	supieron

TENER TO HAVE

tuve	tuvimos
tuviste	tuvisteis
tuvo	tuvieron

TRAER TO BRING

traje	trajimos
trajiste	trajisteis
trajo	trajeron

VENIR TO COME

vine	vinimos
viniste	vinisteis
vino	vinieron

ANDAR TO WALK

anduve	anduvimos
anduviste	anduvisteis
anduvo	anduvieron

CABER TO FIT

cupe	cupimos
cupiste	cupisteis
cupo	cupieron

PRODUCIR TO PRODUCE

produje	produjimos
produjiste	produjisteis
produjo	produjeron

Note the endings of **dar** and **ver**:

DAR TO GIVE

di	dimos
diste	disteis
dio	dieron

VER TO SEE

vi	vimos
viste	visteis
vio	vieron

Note: Verbs whose irregular stem ends in **-j** in the preterit have the ending **-eron** instead of **-ieron** in the third-person plural: **dijeron, produjeron, trajeron.**

■ The verbs **ser** *(to be)* and **ir** *(to go)* have the same conjugation in the preterit tense. The context of the sentence usually makes it clear which of the verbs is meant:

SER TO BE / IR TO GO

fui	fuimos
fuiste	fuisteis
fue	fueron

■ The preterit of **hay** (from the verb **haber**) is **hubo.**

E. ¡Qué fiesta más divertida! Tell about the party you attended last night. Rewrite the following sentences in the preterit tense.

Modelo   Todos están contentos. ➤ Todos estuvieron contentos.

1. Hay una fiesta en casa de Rosaura Mondragón.

   Hubo una fiesta en casa de Rosaura Mondragón

2. Los padres de Rosaura dan la fiesta.

   Los padres de Rosaura dieron la fiesta

3. Hacen muchos platos interesantes.

   Hicieron muchos platos interesantes

4. Toda la comida está rica.

   Toda la comida estuvo rica

5. Todos nosotros traemos regalos.

   Todos nosotros trajimos regalos

6. Yo veo a mis amigos.

   Yo vi a mis amigos

7. Va Beatriz, pero no puede ir su hermana.

   Va Beatriz, pero no pudo ir su hermana

8. Yo les digo "gracias por todo" a los Mondragón.

   Yo les dije "gracias por todo" a los Mondragón

F. ¿Adónde fueron? Tell where everyone went by writing sentences with the verb **ir** in the preterit and the cues.

Modelo   Uds. / el campo ➤ Uds. fueron al campo.

1. yo / el teatro   *Yo fui el teatro*

2. Rosario y Daniel / el supermercado   *Rosario y Daniel fueron supermercado*

3. tú / la tienda de discos   *Tú fuiste la tienda de discos*

4. Sergio y yo / unas librerías   *Sergio y yo fuimos unas librerías*

5. Ud. / el acuario   *Ud. fue el acuario*

6. Esmeralda / la peluquería   *Esmeralda fue la peluquería*

7. vosotras / la dentista   *Vosotras fuisteis la dentista*

G. **Diálogos.** Complete the following dialogues by writing the correct preterit forms of the verbs in parentheses.

1. —¿Quién _____tuvo_____ la idea? (tener)

2. —Creo que _____fue_____ Luis Fernando. (ser)

3. —_____hizo_____ frío ayer, ¿verdad? (hacer)

4. —Sí, _____hizo_____ 25 grados y _____estuvo_____ nublado.
   (hacer / estar)

5. —¿Cómo _____supiste_____ tú lo que pasó? (saber)

6. —Me lo _____dije_____ mis amigos. (decir)

7. —Uds. no _____vinieron_____ a vernos el sábado. (venir)

8. —Es que nosotros no _____pudimos_____ ir. (poder)

H. **Ayer fue diferente.** People do certain things every day, but yesterday they didn't do them. Explain what didn't happen. Write sentences with verbs in the preterit and change direct object nouns to pronouns whenever possible.

Modelo Los niños almuerzan a la una todos los días.
➤ Pero ayer no almorzaron a la una.

1. Andamos por la plaza todos los días.

   Pero ayer no la andamos

2. Raquel ve a sus amigos todos los días.

   Pero ayer Raquel no los vio

3. Traigo manzanas todos los días.

   Pero ayer no las traje

4. Uds. ponen la mesa todos los días.

   Pero ayer no la pusieron

5. Vas a la biblioteca todos los días.

   Pero ayer no la fuiste

6. Ud. viene en autobús todos los días.

   Pero ayer no lo vino

7. Ricardo y Esteban conducen en la carretera todos los días.

   Pero ayer Ricardo y Esteban no la condujeron

8. Hacéis pan todos los días.

   Pero ayer no hicisteis pan

II. *Hace* + Expression of Time + *que* + Verb in the Preterit

Hace + expression of time + **que** + verb in the preterit tense means *ago*.
When the expression is used in questions, the word **tiempo** can be omitted:

> —¿Cuánto (tiempo) hace que   *"How long ago did you live in*
>   vivió Ud. en Chile?   *Chile?"*
> —Hace diez años que viví en Chile. ⎱
> —Viví en Chile hace diez años. ⎰ *"I lived in Chile ten years ago."*

I. **Hace... que yo...** Answer the following questions by using the construction
hace + expression of time + **que** + verb in the preterit tense and the cues
given in parentheses. Change direct object nouns to pronouns whenever
possible.

Modelo   —¿Cuánto tiempo hace que cenaste? (media hora)
        ➤ —Hace media hora que cené.

1. —¿Cuánto tiempo hace que celebraste tu cumpleaños? (cuatro meses)

   Hace cuatro meses que yo celebré mi cumpleaños

2. —¿Cuánto tiempo hace que Uds. tomaron química? (dos años)

   Hace dos años que nosotros tomamos química

3. —¿Cuánto tiempo hace que Alejo y Felipe jugaron ese videojuego?
   (una semana)

   Hace una semana que Alejo y Felipe jugaron ese videojuego

4. —¿Cuánto tiempo hace que Ud. vino a esta ciudad? (un año)

   Hace un año que yo vine a esta ciudad

5. —¿Cuánto tiempo hace que pagué las cuentas? (varios días)

   Hace varios días que yo pagué las cuentas

6. —¿Cuánto tiempo hace que llegó Natalia? (un par de horas)

   Hace un par de horas que Natalia llegó

J. **Preguntas personales.** Answer the following questions in complete Spanish sentences.

1. ¿Qué hiciste ayer?

   Yo hice la tarea anoche

2. ¿Adónde fuiste el fin de semana pasado?

   _____

3. ¿Con quiénes saliste?

   _____

4. ¿Qué comiste y bebiste hoy?

   _____

5. ¿Cuánto hace que viajaste a otro país o a otra ciudad? ¿Adónde fuiste?

   _____

6. ¿Cuánto hace que conociste a tu mejor amigo/amiga?

   _____

K. **Composición.** Write eight to ten sentences in a travel log giving the details of a trip you took. Include where and when you went, what you saw and did, how you traveled, with whom you went, what you bought, and other details. Use as many verbs as you can in the preterit tense.

The Imperfect Tense;
The Imperfect vs. the Preterit

I. The Imperfect Tense

■ The imperfect tense is used to express an event or action that was going on in the past, without any reference to its beginning or end. The imperfect is the tense used for description and expressing background in the past. It is also the tense used to express repeated actions in the past. The imperfect is commonly expressed in English as *used to do* or *was doing*.

■ Adverbs and adverbial phrases such as **siempre** and **todos los días** are often clues for the use of the imperfect rather than the preterit tense.

■ The imperfect tense is formed by adding the imperfect-tense endings to the stem of the verb. Study the following conjugations:

TOMAR *TO TAKE*

yo tom**aba**	nosotros/nosotras tom**ábamos**
tú tom**abas**	vosotros/vosotras tom**abais**
él ⎫	ellos ⎫
ella ⎬ tom**aba**	ellas ⎬ tom**aban**
Ud. ⎭	Uds. ⎭

COMER *TO EAT*

yo com**ía**	nosotros/nosotras com**íamos**
tú com**ías**	vosotros/vosotras com**íais**
él ⎫	ellos ⎫
ella ⎬ com**ía**	ellas ⎬ com**ían**
Ud. ⎭	Uds. ⎭

VIVIR *TO LIVE*

yo viv**ía**	nosotros/nosotras viv**íamos**
tú viv**ías**	vosotros/vosotras viv**íais**
él ⎫	ellos ⎫
ella ⎬ viv**ía**	ellas ⎬ viv**ían**
Ud. ⎭	Uds. ⎭

—Yo tomaba el tren de cercanías. ¿Y tú?	*"I used to take the commuter train. What about you?"*
—Yo vivía muy cerca y caminaba todos los días.	*"I lived close by and walked every day."*
—¿Qué hacían Uds. en el centro?	*"What were you doing downtown?"*
—Nos paseábamos.	*"We were walking around."*

Notes:

1. For **gustar** and the verbs that follow the same pattern, the imperfect endings are -**aba** and -**aban: nos gustaba, le gustaban.**

2. **Hay,** which comes from the verb **haber,** is **había** in the imperfect tense.

■ All verbs are regular in the imperfect tense with the exception of **ir, ser,** and **ver:**

IR *TO GO*

yo **iba**	nosotros/nosotras **íbamos**
tú **ibas**	vosotros/vosotras **ibais**
él ella Ud. } **iba**	ellos ellas Uds. } **iban**

SER *TO BE*

yo **era**	nosotros/nosotras **éramos**
tú **eras**	vosotros/vosotras **erais**
él ella Ud. } **era**	ellos ellas Uds. } **eran**

VER *TO SEE*

yo **veía**	nosotros/nosotras **veíamos**
tú **veías**	vosotros/vosotras **veíais**
él ella Ud. } **veía**	ellos ellas Uds. } **veían**

Siempre íbamos al circo y veíamos los elefantes.	*We always went to the circus and saw the elephants.*
Era un día maravilloso de verano.	*It was a wonderful summer day.*

■ The imperfect tense is the only tense used to state the time in the past:

—**¿Qué hora era cuando regresaron?**	*"What time was it when they came back?"*
—**Eran las diez y media.**	*"It was 10:30."*

A. ¿Qué hacían? Describe what people were doing a few weekends ago. Use the cues to write sentences in the imperfect tense.

Modelo   Eunice / estudiar para un examen
➤ Eunice estudiaba para un examen.

1. Manolo y Benito / jugar al baloncesto

   Manolo y Benito jugaban al baloncesto

2. tú / leer el periódico

   Tú leías el periódico

3. nosotros / dar un paseo

   Nosotros dábamos un paseo

4. Sara / correr en el parque

   Sara corría en el parque

5. yo / escribir cartas

   Yo escribía cartas

6. Uds. / escuchar discos compactos

   Uds. escuchaban discos compactos

7. Ud. / ver televisión

   Ud. veía televisión

8. vosotros / ir a los museos de arte

   Vosotros ibais a los museos de arte

B. Cuando estaba de vacaciones... Felipe remembers his childhood vacations fondly. Find out why by writing sentences with the verbs in the imperfect.

Modelo   yo / pasarlo muy bien ➤ Lo pasaba muy bien.

Frases útiles

el coche todo terreno _jeep_

hacer diligencias _to do/run errands_

el picazón _insect bite_

---

1. yo / gustar dormir hasta las once

   Yo gustaba dormir hasta las once

2. mis amigos y yo / encantar ir al parque todos los días

   Mis amigos y yo encantábamos ir al parque todos los días

3. nosotros / sufrir de picazones

   Nosotros sufríamos de picazones

➤➤➤➤➤

4. yo / hacer diligencias para mi mamá

Yo hacía diligencias para mi mamá

5. mis compañeros y yo / ir al cine los sábados

Mis compañeras y yo ibamos al cine los sábados

6. Pepe y yo / jugar videojuegos

Pepe y yo jugábamos videojuegos

7. nosotros / aprender a tocar la guitarra

nosotros aprendíamos a tocar la guitarra

8. yo / conducir nuestro coche todo terreno

Yo conducía nuestro coche todo terreno

C. ¿Todo sigue igual? Bernardo meets an acquaintance he hasn't seen in a year. He answers this person's questions by saying that things used to be a certain way, but no longer are. Write Bernardo's reponses in the imperfect tense.

Modelo —Cursas física, ¿no?
➤ —Cursaba física, pero ya no.

1. —Estudias para ingeniero, ¿no?

—*Estudiaba para ingeniero, pero ya no*

2. —Uds. viven en las afueras, ¿no?

—*Vivíamos en la afueras, pero ya no*

3. —Sales con Marisol del Valle, ¿no?

—*Salía con Marisol de Valle, pero ya no*

4. —Tu hermana es programadora, ¿no?

—*Mi hermana era programadora, pero ya no*

5. —Tus primos juegan en un equipo de fútbol, ¿no?

—*Mis primos jugaban en un equipo de fútbol, pero ya no*

6. —Trabajas con tus amigos en la gasolinera, ¿no?

—*Trabajaba con mis amigos en la gasolinera, pero ya no*

7. —Uds. van a la costa en agosto, ¿no?

   —*Ibamos a la costa en agosto, pero ya no*

8. —Te gusta probar restaurantes nuevos, ¿no?

   —*Me gustaba probar restaurantes nuevos, pero ya no*

II. The Imperfect vs. the Preterit

■ The imperfect and the preterit tenses express different ways of looking at past actions and events. The imperfect designates an action going on in the past without reference to its beginning or end, but the preterit designates an action as completed in the past. These differences are sometimes, but not always, evident in English:

Cuando Mateo trabajaba en esa empresa, viajaba todos los meses.	*When Mateo worked at that firm, he traveled (used to travel) every month.*
Mateo viajó a Honduras el mes pasado.	*Mateo traveled to Honduras last month.*
Irene compró dulces mientras yo hacía ejercicio.	*Irene bought candy while I was exercising.*
Estabas en el sótano cuando Elisa llamó a la puerta.	*You were in the basement when Elisa knocked on the door.*

■ For some Spanish verbs, the difference between the imperfect and the preterit can be seen in the meaning of the verb:

saber *to know*

Sabía su dirección.	*I knew his address.*
Supe su dirección.	*I found out his address.*

conocer *to know*

Conocías a Tere, ¿no?	*You knew Tere, didn't you?*
Conociste a Tere, ¿no?	*You met Tere, didn't you?*

tener *to have*

Teníamos una idea.	*We had an idea.*
Tuvimos una idea.	*We got an idea.*

poder *to be able*

No podían subir al tren.	*They couldn't get on the train.*
No pudieron subir al tren.	*They couldn't (didn't manage to) get on the train.*

querer *to want*

No querían pagar con tarjeta de crédito.	*They didn't want to pay with a credit card.*
No quisieron pagar con tarjeta de crédito.	*They refused to (didn't want to and didn't) pay with a credit card.*

D. No hacía... cuando... Say that the weather was not as it is now when certain things occurred. Write sentences using the imperfect to talk about the weather and the preterit to tell what happened.

Modelo   Hace frío. yo / entrar en la casa
➢ No hacía frío cuando entré en la casa.

1. Está nublado. nosotros / llegar a la playa

   No estaba nublado cuando llegamos a la playa

2. Hace buen tiempo. los niños / salir al patio

   No hacía buen tiempo cuando salieron al patio

3. Llueve. tú / venir a vernos   llover → llovía

   No (llueve) cuando veniste a vernos

4. Hace sol. yo / barrer el patio

   No hacía sol cuando barrí el patio

5. Nieva. José Gabriel / estacionar el coche

   No nieva cuando José Gabriel estacionó el coche

6. Hace mucho viento. Uds. / ir al aeropuerto

   No hacía mucho viento cuando fueron al aeropuerto

E. ¿Qué hora era cuando...? Tell at what time certain things happened today. Write sentences using the imperfect to tell time and the preterit for the completed action.

Modelo   2:00 P.M. / llegar el cartero
➢ Eran las dos de la tarde cuando llegó el cartero.

1. 9:00 A.M. / sonar el teléfono

   Eran las nueve de la mañana cuando sonó el teléfono

2. 11:30 P.M. / yo / terminar el proyecto

   Eran las once y media de la tarde cuando yo terminé el proyecto

3. 8:15 A.M. / Bárbara / ver el accidente

   Eran las ocho y cuarto cuando Brandon vio el accidente

+4

+5

4. 1:45 P.M. / Uds. / poner la mesa

Eran las dos menos cuarto cuando pusieron la mesa

5. 5:00 P.M. / tú / llevar a tus padres al restaurante

Eran las cinco cuando llevaste a tus padres al restaurante

6. 10:00 P.M. / nosotros / ir a la discoteca

Eran las diez cuando fuimos a la discoteca

F. La vida de Fernando Montemayor. Complete the following paragraph about Fernando Montemayor's life. Write either the preterit or the imperfect of the verbs in parentheses.

Estudios y amor

administrar *to manage, to run*	**el olivo** *olive tree*
el ganado *livestock*	**el recinto universitario** *college campus*
el noviazgo *courtship*	**el trigo** *wheat*

Fernando Montemayor ___nacía___ (1. nacer) en Mérida. Sus

padres ___eran___ (2. ser) dueños de una hacienda muy grande. Ellos

___cultivaron___ (3. cultivar) olivos y trigo y ___tenía___ (4. tener)

mucho ganado también. Fernando ___era___ (5. ser) inteligente

y ___sacaba___ (6. sacar) buenas notas en el colegio.

Él ___decidía___ (7. decidir) cuando ___era___ (8. ser) pequeño

que ___iba___ (9. ir) a estudiar agricultura en la universidad. Cuando

___tenía___ (10. tener) 19 años, ___fue___ (11. ir) a la

universidad en Madrid. Fernando ___vivía___ (12. vivir) muy cerca

del recinto universitario. Él ___estaba___ (13. estar) muy contento.

Allí ___conoció___ (14. conocer) a Beatriz Morella que ___estudiaba___

(15. estudiar) economía. Durante el noviazgo, Fernando le ___describió___

(16. describir) la hacienda en Extremadura y le ___contró___ (17. contar)

sus sueños de algún día administrar las tierras de su familia.

Extremadura

■ **Extremadura** is a natural region in Spain as well as a regional autonomous government (**comunidad autónoma**). Extremadura is bordered by Portugal to the west, Andalucía to the south, Castilla la Nueva to the east, and the province of Salamanca to the north. Extremadura means **"más allá del Duero"** (the land beyond the Duero River), a name dating back to the Reconquest (**la Reconquista**), which was the period from the eighth through the fifteenth centuries during which Christians fought to drive the Arabs out of Spain.

■ This region, far from the centers of culture and industry, is a vast plateau with an austere landscape. Agriculture is the mainstay of the economy, particularly along the Guadiana and Alagón rivers where wheat, olives, fruits and vegetables, tobacco, and cotton are grown. Also important are the production of cork and sheep and pig raising.

■ **Mérida,** the capital of Extremadura, was founded in 25 B.C. by the Romans. Located on the Guadiana River and situated at the junction of major Roman roads between Salamanca and Sevilla and Toledo and Lisbon, Mérida became an important center. Among the attraction for visitors are wonderful Roman ruins, such as the theater (**teatro romano**) and the arena (**el anfiteatro**), as well as the superb **Museo Nacional de Arte Romano.**

G. Un vuelo lento *(A slow flight)*. Tell about Margarita Alonso's plane trip. Write either the imperfect or the preterit tense of the verbs in parentheses.

El avión

el/la auxiliar de vuelo *flight attendant*

el despegue *takeoff*

facturar *to check*

la puerta *gate*

el retraso *delay*

la tarjeta de embarque *boarding pass*

Ya _____ (1. ser) tarde cuando yo _____

(2. llegar) a las Aerolíneas Espanaire. Le _____ (3. mostrar)

mi billete al agente y él me _____ (4. dar) una tarjeta de

embarque. Yo _____ (5. facturar) mi equipaje y

_____ (6. ir) corriendo a la puerta. _____ (7. Haber)

muchos pasajeros esperando. Todos _____ (8. hacer) cola.

Por fin nosotros _____ (9. subir) al avión. Un auxiliar de

vuelo me _____ (10. enseñar) mi asiento. El asiento

_____ (11. estar) junto a la ventanilla. ¡Qué hermoso

_____ (12. ser) el panorama! Yo _____ (13. sacar)

mi computadora portátil y _____ (14. tener) ganas de estar

en el aire ya. Todos nosotros _____ (15. esperar) el despegue.

_____ (16. Pasar) unos minutos cuando nosotros

_____ (17. oír) la voz del piloto. Él _____

(18. decir): "¡Retraso de dos horas!"

H. Una tarde en el parque. Tell how Antonio and his friends spent the afternoon in the park. Write sentences with the verbs in the imperfect or the preterit.

Modelo   Antonio y sus amigos / ir al parque a las once de la mañana
➤ Antonio y sus amigos fueron al parque a las once de la mañana.

1. hacer / muy buen tiempo

   _____

2. hacer / sol y calor

   _____

3. haber / mucha gente en el parque

   _____

4. los amigos / pensar pasar una hora allí

   _____

5. los chicos / jugar un partido de fútbol

   _____

6. ¡qué emocionante / estar el partido!

   _____

7. después / los chicos / comer un helado

   _____

8. ser / las tres de la tarde / cuando / Antonio / volver a casa

   _____

I. Preguntas personales. Answer the following questions in complete Spanish sentences.

1. ¿Cuántos años tenías cuando comenzaste a estudiar español?

   _____

2. ¿Cómo eras de niño/niña?

   _____

3. ¿Qué te gustaba hacer cuando eras niño/niña?

   _____

4. ¿Qué tiempo hacía cuando saliste de casa hoy?

   _____

5. ¿Qué cosas hacías que ya no te interesan ahora? ¿Qué cosas haces ahora que no te interesaban antes?

   _____

   _____

J. Composición. Write eight to ten sentences telling what you did and saw while you were on vacation. Select the imperfect or the preterit tense for each verb you use.

I. Commands: *Ud., Uds.*

- The command forms of a verb are used to tell someone to do or not to do something. The forms of the formal commands (for **Ud.** and **Uds.**) are derived from the **yo** form of the present tense for regular, stem-changing, and irregular verbs. For -**ar** verbs, the present-tense endings -**a** and -**an** become -**e** and -**en**. For -**er** and -**ir** verbs, the present-tense endings -**e** and -**en** become -**a** and -**an**:

Maneje con cuidado.	*Drive carefully.*
Aprenda lo más posible.	*Learn as much as possible.*
Asistan al concierto.	*Attend/Go to the concert.*
Tengan cuidado.	*Be careful.*

- For -**ar** verbs whose stems end in **c, g,** or **z,** you change the **c** to **qu,** the **g** to **gu,** and the **z** to **c** before adding the command endings -**e** and -**en**:

Saque billetes.	*Get tickets.*
Llegue temprano.	*Come early.*
Empiecen a comer.	*Start to eat.*

- Negative commands are formed by the addition of **no** before the affirmative command:

No regrese tarde.	*Don't come back late.*
No abran este paquete.	*Don't open this package.*

- A tone of politeness can soften the command by the addition of **Ud.** or **Uds.** This is the same as using *please* in English commands:

Mire. / Mire Ud.	*Look. / Please look.*
No esperen. / No esperen Uds.	*Don't wait. / Please don't wait.*

A. La ofimática *(Office technology).* Write sentences using **Ud.** commands to explain to a new office employee some of the operations he must or must not perform on his computer.

Modelo limpiar la pantalla ➤ Limpie la pantalla.

La computadora	
borrar *to delete*	**hacer clic del ratón** *to click on the mouse*
crear una carpeta *to create a file*	
el disquete *diskette*	**navegar** *to surf*
guardar los datos *to keep, save the data*	**la pantalla** *screen*
	teclear *to type*

1. entrar en el Internet   *Entre en el internet*

2. navegar en el web   *Navegue en el web*

3. hacer clic del ratón   *Haga clic del ratón*

4. no borrar estos mensajes   *No borre estos mensajes*

5. escribir la dirección electrónica   *Escriba la dirrección electrónica*

6. enviar mensajes   *envie mensajes*

7. no teclear tan fuerte   *no teclee tan fuerte*

8. abrir la ventana   *abra la ventana*

9. meter el disquete   *meta el disquete*

10. crear una carpeta   *cree una carpeta*

11. guardar los datos   *guarde los datos*

12. no mover el cursor   *no mova el curso*

13. no salir todavía   *no salga todavía*

B. ¡Qué rico! Tell your friends how to make the Spanish dessert **manzanas asadas con miel** (baked apples with honey). To follow the recipe, change the infinitive of the verbs to the **Uds.** form of the command.

Modelo   comprar seis manzanas ➤ Compren seis manzanas.

Una receta: Manzanas asadas con miel

la almendra *almond*	**mezclar** *to mix*
el higo *fig*	**la nata batida** *whipped cream*
el jerez *sherry*	**picar** *to chop*
llenar *to fill*	**quitar el corazón** *to core*

---

1. quitar el corazón de las manzanas

   Quiten el corazón de las manzanas

2. picar una taza de higos y almendras

   Picuen una taza de higos y alemendras

3. llenar las manzanas con los higos y las almendras

   Llenen las manzanas con los higos y las alemandras

4. mezclar una taza de miel, una cucharadita de mantequilla y media taza de jerez

   Mezclen una taza de miel, una cucharadita de mantequilla y media taza de jerez

5. añadir la mezcla a las manzanas

   Añadan la mezcla a las manzanas

   $+\dfrac{2}{2}$

6. cocinar las manzanas en el horno

   Cocinen las manzanas en el horno

7. sacar las manzanas del horno

   Saquen las manzanas del horno

8. servir las manzanas con nata batida

   Sirvan las manzanas con nata batida

II. Commands: *tú*

- The affirmative informal commands for **tú** are derived from the **tú** form in the present tense, minus the ending **-s.** In other words, the **tú** commands are the same as the third-person singular form of the present tense:

present tense	*tú* command
Viajas en julio.	**Viaja en julio.** *Travel in July.*
Lees esta novela.	**Lee esta novela.** *Read this novel.*
Decides hoy.	**Decide hoy.** *Decide today.*
Piensas en el asunto.	**Piensa en el asunto.** *Think about the matter.*

- Negative **tú** commands are the same as the **Ud.** commands plus the ending **-s:**

Ud. command	*tú* command
Alquile una película.	**No alquiles una película.** *Don't rent a film.*
Corra rápido.	**No corras rápido.** *Don't run quickly.*
Abra la caja.	**No abras la caja.** *Don't open the box.*
Salga ahora.	**No salgas ahora.** *Don't leave now.*
Juegue al golf.	**No juegues al golf.** *Don't play golf.*

- Some verbs have irregular affirmative **tú** command forms. However, these verbs have regular negative **tú** commands:

verb	affirmative *tú* command	negative *tú* command
decir	**di**	**no digas**
hacer	**haz**	**no hagas**
ir	**ve**	**no vayas**
poner	**pon**	**no pongas**
salir	**sal**	**no salgas**
ser	**sé**	**no seas**
tener	**ten**	**no tengas**
venir	**ven**	**no vengas**

Di algo.   *Say something.*
No digas nada.   *Don't say anything.*

Note: The affirmative **tú** commands for **ir** and **ver** are the same: **ve.**

C. **Una estación de invierno *(A winter resort).*** Pilar Álvarez writes a letter to her friend Paloma Sanz to invite her to go skiing with her and her family. Find out what Pilar tells her friend by changing the infinitives to **tú** commands.

Modelo   visitar la estación de invierno ➤ Visita la estación de invierno.

Querida Paloma:

Si no tienes planes, ___*pasa*___ (1. pasar) las vacaciones

conmigo. ___*Viene*___ (2. Venir) a mi casa en Tarragona. Luego

___*ve*___ (3. ir) con nosotros a una estación de invierno de los

Pirineos. _esquía_ (4. Esquiar) con nosotros en Andorra y Baqueira.

habla (5. Hablar) con tus padres hoy. Si te dejan ir,

sal (6. salir) de Alicante en tren el sábado. ~~_oye_~~

(7. Oír) chica, _dile_ (8. decir) que sí. _saca_

(9. Sacar) los esquíes del armario y _haz_ (10. hacer) la maleta hoy

mismo. Y no _olvides_ (11. olvidar) el traje de baño y un traje de

vestir. _recuerda_ (12. Recordar) que hay piscina y discoteca también.

Paloma, no _esperes_ (13. esperar) ni un minuto más.

trata (14. Tratar) de convencer a tus papás ahora mismo.

Turismo en España

- **Alicante,** the capital of the province of Alicante in the Levante region, is an important commercial and industrial city and Mediterranean port. Because of its brilliant skies, the Greeks called Alicante "the white citadel," and the Romans called it "the city of light." Its great stretches of beach have made Alicante the resort center of **la Costa Blanca.**
- **Tarragona** is a city in Catalonia (**Cataluña**) to the south of Barcelona on the part of the Mediterranean called **la Costa Dorada** (Golden Coast). The Romans developed Tarraconensis into a major city and port in the first and second centuries B.C. Tarragona is a modern, beautiful city rich in Roman ruins and medieval structures.
- **Andorra,** in the heart of the Pyrenees Mountains, has Catalonia to the south and France to the north. Only 181 square miles in area, it is a parliamentary co-principality, with the President of France and the Bishop of Urgel (Spain) as its heads of state. Andorra had been an independent principality with joint sovereignty by Spain and France from 1278 to 1993. In 1993, Andorran citizens voted to end the feudal system and adopt a parliamentary system of government. **Catalán** is the official language, but Spanish and French are also spoken. The economy of Andorra is based primarily on tourism, with about 13 million tourists visiting annually to take advantage of its status as a free port and to enjoy its many spectacular ski resorts.
- **Baqueira** is considered the best and most fashionable ski resort center in the Spanish Pyrenees and one of the busiest and most exciting in all of Europe. In addition to its well-equipped skiing facilities, it has indoor and outdoor pools, tennis courts, gyms, restaurants, and dance clubs. The annual Spanish dogsled championship goes through Baqueira, Pas de la Casa in Andorra, and other Pyrenees resorts.

III. *Nosotros* Commands

- The command forms for **nosotros** *(let's, let's not)* are derived from the **yo** form of the present tense for regular and irregular verbs. The ending **-emos** is used for **-ar** verbs and the ending **-amos** is used for **-er** and **-ir** verbs: **hablo** ➤ **hablemos, como** ➤ **comamos, abro** ➤ **abramos, tengo** ➤ **tengamos, digo** ➤ **digamos**:

Tomemos una limonada.	*Let's have a lemonade.*
No salgamos todavía.	*Let's not go out yet.*

- For stem-changing verbs, the **nosotros** commands are made from the **nosotros** form of the present tense. Note that **-ir** verbs that change **e** ➤ **ie** or **e** ➤ **i** in the present tense also have **i** as the stem vowel in the **nosotros** form of the command; **dormir** and **morir** have **u** as the stem vowel:

Pensemos bien de los demás.	*Let's think well of others.*
No sirvamos arroz con pollo.	*Let's not serve chicken and rice.*
Durmamos un rato más.	*Let's sleep a while longer.*

- **-Ar** verbs whose stems end in **c, g,** or **z** have the usual spelling changes before the command ending **-emos:** **c** ➤ **qu, g** ➤ **gu, z** ➤ **c:**

Busquemos estacionamiento.	*Let's look for a parking spot.*
No juguemos al tenis hoy.	*Let's not play tennis today.*
Comencemos la lección.	*Let's begin the lesson.*

- The affirmative **nosotros** command can be replaced by **vamos a** + infinitive. **Vamos a comer** means either *Let's eat* or *We're going to eat.* **No vamos a comer** can only mean *We're not going to eat:*

Esperemos un rato.	
Vamos a esperar un rato.	*Let's wait a while.*

Note: Vamos, not **vayamos,** is used for *let's go,* but Spanish uses **no vayamos** for *let's not go.*

D. De dos maneras. Silvia wants to do several things today. Her friends are happy to join her. First write their responses, using **nosotros** commands. Then write each response using **vamos a** + infinitive.

Modelo —Quiero aprovechar el día.
     ➤ —Aprovechemos el día.
     ➤ —Vamos a aprovechar el día.

1. —Quiero alquilar esta película.

  — _____

  — _____

2. —Quiero dar un paseo.

— _____

— _____

3. —Quiero almorzar al aire libre.

— _____

— _____

4. —Quiero comer en el restaurante colombiano.

— _____

— _____

5. —Quiero abrir todas las ventanas.

— _____

— _____

6. —Quiero ver la exposición de arte moderno.

— _____

— _____

IV. Position of Object Pronouns with Commands

■ Object pronouns (direct, indirect, and reflexive) are placed in their usual position before the verb in negative commands. (See Chapter 11 for direct and indirect object pronouns and Chapter 16 for reflexive verbs and pronouns.)

No los lleve.	*Don't take them.*
No se lo digan.	*Don't tell it to her.*
No nos la pidas.	*Don't ask us for it.*
No te quedes.	*Don't stay.*
No se vayan Uds.	*Please don't go/leave.*
No te pongas las botas.	*Don't put the boots on.*
No te las pongas.	*Don't put them on.*

- Object pronouns follow affirmative commands and are attached to them. When they are attached, an accent mark is placed over the stressed syllable, except when a single object pronoun is added to a one-syllable command form: **dime** *(tell me)* but **dímelo** *(tell me it)*:

Llévelos.	*Take them.*
Díganselo.	*Tell it to her.*
Pídenosla.	*Ask us for it.*
Quédate.	*Stay.*
Váyanse Uds.	*Please go/leave.*
Ponte las botas.	*Put on the boots.*
Póntelas.	*Put them on.*

Note: Dé (the **Ud.** command for *give*) may or may not keep its accent mark when a single object pronoun is added. Both forms, **déme** and **deme,** are commonly found in writing.

- In affirmative **nosotros** commands, the final **-s** of the verb ending is dropped when the reflexive pronoun **nos** or the indirect object pronoun **se** is added. An accent mark is written over the stressed syllable:

Sentemos + nos = **Sentémonos.** *(Let's sit down.)*
Demos + se + los = **Démoselos.** *(Let's give them to him.)*

(quedarse)	**Quedémonos.**	*Let's stay.*
(irse)	**Vámonos.**	*Let's go.*
(traérsela)	**Traigámosela.**	*Let's bring it to them.*

E. Verbos reflexivos. Write affirmative or negative commands for **tú, Ud.,** or **Uds.** from the reflexive verbs given.

1. alegrarse / tú   _____

2. no asustarse / Ud.   _____

3. reunirse / Uds.   _____

4. no irse / tú   _____

5. ponerse en forma / Uds. _____

6. acordarse / Ud.   _____

7. despertarse / tú   _____

8. no hacerse daño / Uds.   _____

9. vestirse / Ud.   _____

F. El imperativo: *Ud., Uds.* Answer each of the following questions with an affirmative and a negative command for **Ud.** or **Uds.** Change direct object nouns to pronouns and make all necessary changes.

Modelo   —¿Le mando las tarjetas (a Ud.)?
     ➤ —Sí, mándemelas.
     ➤ —No, no me las mande.

1. —¿Les muestro mi nuevo cartel (a Uds.)?

— _Sí, muéstrenoslo_

— _No, no nos lo muestre_

2. —¿Les ponemos los zapatos a los niños?

— _Sí, pónganleslos_

— _No, no les los pongan_

3. —¿Le doy la agenda a Julia?

— _Sí, dóyelela_

— _No, no le la doye_

4. —¿Le explicamos nuestras ideas (a Ud.)?

— _Sí, explíquenmelas_

— _No, no me las expliquen_

5. —¿Les devuelvo los informes a los jefes?

— _Sí, dévuelvaleslos_

— _No, no les los devuelva_

G. El imperativo: *tú*. Answer each of the following questions with an affirmative and a negative command for **tú.** Change direct object nouns to pronouns and make all necessary changes.

Modelo   —¿Te preparo la ensalada?
➤ —Sí, prepáramela.
➤ —No, no me la prepares.

1. —¿Te presto los libros de consulta?
— Sí, préstámelos
— No, no me los prestes

2. —¿Les llevo las revistas a tus hermanos?
— Sí, llévaleslas
— No, no les las lleves

3. —¿Te sirvo un bocadillo?
— Sí, sírvemelo
— No, no me lo sirvas

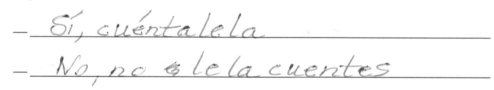

4. —¿Le cuento la historia a Manuela?
— Sí, cuéntalela
— No, no se le la cuentes

5. —¿Te hago la reservación?
— Sí, házmela
— No, no me la hagas

H. Preguntas personales. Answer the following questions in complete Spanish sentences.

1. ¿Sabes entrar en el Internet y navegar en el web? ¿Qué mandatos *(commands)* usas?

   _____

2. ¿Qué plato especial sabes preparar? ¿Cómo es la receta?

   _____

3. ¿Qué dices para invitar a tus amigos a ir al cine / a una fiesta / a esquiar?

   _____

4. Tu hermanito no quiere obedecerte. ¿Qué le dices?

   _____

   _____

I. Composición. Choose a topic and write a dialogue of eight to ten sentences in which two people use command forms. Be sure to select the correct form (**Ud.** or **tú**) of the command for the person addressed in the given situation. Possible situations include the following: a friend advises another friend about what clothing to buy on a shopping trip; a parent gives advice to his or her son or daughter; a doctor makes recommendations to a patient; a teacher instructs his or her student in a particular subject matter.

Reflexive Verbs; Reflexive Verbs with Reciprocal Meaning; The Impersonal Use of se; "To Become" in Spanish

I. Reflexive Verbs

■ Many verbs in Spanish always have a reflexive pronoun (in English, a pronoun that ends in *-self* or *-selves*) that refers to or reflects back on the person or thing that is the subject. The reflexive pronouns in Spanish are **me, te, se, nos, os, se.** Verbs that always have a reflexive pronoun are called *reflexive verbs.*

■ Most Spanish reflexive verbs correspond to English verbs that do not have a direct object (called *intransitive verbs*) or to English verb phrases with *to be* or *to get* + an adjective, an adverb, or a past participle: **alegrarse** *(to be glad, happy)*, **levantarse** *(to get up).*

■ Reflexive verbs are conjugated in all tenses. They can be regular, irregular, stem-changing, or have changes in spelling. The only difference is the reflexive pronoun, which precedes the conjugated verb form. Study the following conjugations:

ALEGRARSE *TO BE GLAD, HAPPY*

yo **me** alegro	nosotros/nosotras **nos** alegramos
tú **te** alegras	vosotros/vosotras **os** alegráis
él ⎫	ellos ⎫
ella ⎬ **se** alegra	ellas ⎬ **se** alegran
Ud. ⎭	Uds. ⎭

VESTIRSE (e ➤ i) *TO GET DRESSED*

yo **me** visto	nosotros/nosotras **nos** vestimos
tú **te** vistes	vosotros/vosotras **os** vestís
él ⎫	ellos ⎫
ella ⎬ **se** viste	ellas ⎬ **se** visten
Ud. ⎭	Uds. ⎭

Me alegro de verte.	*I'm happy to see you.*
¿No te vistes todavía?	*Aren't you getting dressed yet?*

■ Many commonly used reflexive verbs have to do with daily activities and personal hygiene:

acostarse (o ➤ ue) *to go to bed*	**ducharse** *to take a shower*
afeitarse *to shave*	**lavarse** *to wash up*
bañarse *to take a bath*	**levantarse** *to get up*
cepillarse los dientes/el pelo *to brush one's teeth/hair*	**maquillarse** *to put on makeup*
	peinarse *to comb one's hair*
despertarse (e ➤ ie) *to wake up*	

- Some commonly used reflexive verbs have to do with feelings and emotions:

alegrarse *to be glad, happy*	**molestarse** *to get annoyed*
animarse *to cheer up*	**preocuparse** *to worry*
enfadarse *to get angry*	**tranquilizarse** *to calm down*

- Most reflexive verbs have a corresponding non-reflexive verb in which the subject and the direct object refer to different people or things *(transitive verbs):*

Acuesto a los niños.	*I put the children to bed.*
Me acuesto.	*I go to bed.*
Los niños *levantaron* las manos.	*The children raised their hands.*
Los niños se levantaron temprano.	*The children got up early.*

- Some reflexive verbs have a reflexive pronoun that acts as an indirect object. These verbs also can have a direct object as well:

lavarse + part of the body *to wash*

limpiarse los dientes *to brush one's teeth*

ponerse + article of clothing *to put on*

quitarse + article of clothing *to take off*

romperse + part of the body/article of clothing *to break/to tear*

Mario y Marta se lavan la cara.	*Mario and Marta wash their faces.*
Nos ponemos el abrigo.	*We put on our coats.*

Note: In Spanish, a singular noun is often used for parts of the body and articles of clothing even with plural subjects. Also, in Spanish, the definite article is used to express the English possessive adjective: **Me cepillo los dientes** *(I brush my teeth).*

- In the verb + infinitive construction, the reflexive pronoun may be placed either before the conjugated verb or after the infinitive:

—Vamos a irnos ahora.	*"Let's leave now."*
—Nos vamos a ir ahora.	
—Tú puedes irte. Yo prefiero quedarme.	*"You can leave. I prefer to stay."*
—Tú te puedes ir. Yo me prefiero quedar.	

- When reflexive verbs also have object pronouns, the reflexive pronoun precedes the indirect or direct object pronoun. Study the examples in the present, present progressive, preterit, and imperfect tenses:

Elena se pone los zapatos.	*Elena is putting on her shoes.*
Elena se los pone.	
Elena está poniéndoselos.	*Elena is putting them on.*
Elena se los está poniendo.	
Elena se los puso.	*Elena put them on.*
Elena se los ponía primero.	*Elena used to put them on first.*

■ With affirmative commands, reflexive pronouns are attached to the verb. With negative commands, the reflexive pronoun precedes the verb. In cases where there is more than one pronoun, the order is always reflexive pronoun followed by indirect object pronoun followed by the direct object pronoun:

Váyase.	*Go away.*
Siéntense.	*Sit down.*
Quítate la chaqueta.	*Take off your jacket.*
Quítatela.	*Take it off.*
No te quites la chaqueta.	*Don't take off your jacket.*
No te la quites.	*Don't take it off.*

A. El horario. Write sentences that tell when people do certain things each day. Use the reflexive verbs in the present tense.

Modelo   Timoteo / levantarse / temprano ➤ Timoteo se levanta temprano.

1. Uds. / despertarse / a las siete

_____

2. yo / desayunarse / a las nueve

_____

3. nosotros / cepillarse los dientes / tres veces al día

_____

4. Antonio / afeitarse / por la mañana

_____

5. tú / peinarse / varias veces al día

_____

6. Ud. / lavarse el pelo / todas las noches

_____

7. Carmen y Bárbara / acostarse / a las once y media

_____

8. vosotros / dormirse / después de cenar

_____

El horario

- In Spain and the Spanish American countries, breakfast (**el desayuno**) is eaten at about the same time as in the United States. Unlike the traditional breakfast in the United States, **el desayuno** is light.
- Lunch (**el almuerzo**) in Spanish America is generally eaten between one and two o'clock. In Spain, lunch (**la comida**) was traditionally a heavy meal that was served at home between two and three o'clock. After the meal, people rested or napped before returning to work in the late afternoon. Stores and offices were closed during those hours, which were referred to as **la siesta.** Nowadays, with the ever-increasing pressures of daily life and work, people tend to eat out more in restaurants rather than travel home for the afternoon meal. More stores and offices tend to stay open during the lunchtime hours.
- In Spanish America, dinner (**la cena**) is served around eight o'clock. In Spain, dinner is traditionally served between ten and eleven o'clock.

B. ¡Contesten el teléfono! Nobody is able to answer the telephone. Tell why by writing sentences with the reflexive verbs in the present progressive. Write each sentence two ways: first by attaching the reflexive pronoun to the present participle (do not forget to add the accent mark) and then, by placing the reflexive pronoun before **estar.**

Modelo   Ud. / ducharse
➤ Ud. está duchándose. / Ud. se está duchando.

1. yo / arreglarse

_____

2. Mireya / probarse unos vestidos

_____

3. tú / acostarse

_____

4. nosotros / reunirse

_____

5. Uds. / lavarse el pelo

_____

6. Felipe y Nacho / vestirse

_____

C. **Emociones y sentimientos.** Write sentences with reflexive verbs in the preterit to tell how people reacted when they received some news.

Modelo   Samuel / enojarse ➢ Samuel se enojó.

<table>
<tr><td colspan="2">**¿Cómo reaccionaron? (How did they react?)**</td></tr>
<tr><td>**asustarse** *to get scared*</td><td>**ofenderse** *to get offended, insulted*</td></tr>
<tr><td>**horrorizarse** *to be horrified*</td><td>**sorprenderse** *to be surprised*</td></tr>
</table>

1. yo / alegrarse _____

2. Beatriz / ofenderse _____

3. tú / asustarse _____

4. Gabriela y Paula / sorprenderse _____

5. nosotros / tranquilizarse _____

6. Uds. / enfadarse _____

7. Ud. / molestarse _____

8. vosotros / horrorizarse _____

D. **Mandatos.** Write affirmative commands for **tú, Ud.,** or **Uds.,** using the reflexive verbs given. Change direct object nouns to pronouns and place them accordingly.

Modelos   Ud. / peinarse ➢ Péinese.
          tú / ponerse el sombrero ➢ Póntelo.

1. Uds. / divertirse mucho _____

2. tú / ponerse los calcetines _____

3. Ud. / probarse la camisa _____

4. tú / dormirse _____

5. Uds. / lavarse las manos _____

6. Ud. / quitarse el sombrero _____

7. tú / tranquilizarse _____

E. ¡No lo haga! Write negative commands for **tú, Ud.,** or **Uds.,** using the reflexive verbs given. Change direct object nouns to pronouns and place them accordingly.

Modelo   tú / cansarse ➤ No te canses.

1. Ud. / no enfermarse _____

2. tú / no cortarse la mano _____

3. Uds. / no enojarse _____

4. Ud. / no romperse el pie _____

5. Uds. / no hacerse daño _____

6. tú / no preocuparse _____

7. Ud. / no caerse _____

8. Uds. / no quemarse _____

F. No se mudó, pero... *(He didn't move, but . . .).* Answer each of the following questions using the cue in parentheses to expand the sentence into a verb + infinitive construction. Change direct object nouns to pronouns and make necessary changes.

Modelo   —¿Felipe se mudó? (necesitar)
          ➤ —No, pero necesita mudarse.

1. —¿Berta y Juan José se casaron? (ir a)

   —_____

2. —¿Uds. se reunieron? (pensar)

   —_____

3. —¿Te pusiste la bufanda? (deber)

   —_____

4. —¿Ud. se cepilló los dientes? (tener que)

   —_____

5. —¿Manuel se hizo amigo de Lidia? (querer)

   —_____

6. —¿Yo me enamoré? (esperar)

   —_____

7. —¿Os desayunasteis? (comenzar a)

   —_____

G. **Antes y después.** Complete each of the following sentences by writing the correct preterit forms of the verb. Choose either the reflexive or the transitive form of the verb as you tell if something happened before or after something else.

Modelo   bañar(se): Sara __bañó__ a los niños y después ella __se bañó__ .

1. sentar(se): Los señores _____ a sus amigos a la mesa y después

    ellos _____ .

2. despertar(se): Yo _____ a las ocho y media y

    _____ a mis hermanos a las nueve.

3. vestir(se): La señora Ojeda _____ a su hija y luego ella

    _____ .

4. acostar(se): Uds. _____ , pero primero _____
    a Juanito.

5. peinar(se): Tú _____ a tu hermanito y después

    _____ , ¿no?

6. calmar(se): Nosotros _____ primero y luego

    _____ a los otros.

7. enojar(se): Vosotros _____ y _____ a vuestros
    amigos.

II. Reflexive Verbs with Reciprocal Meaning

■ Reflexive verbs are used in the plural forms to express actions that are reciprocal, expressed in English as *each other* or *one another:*

—¿Uds. se ven de vez en cuando?	*"Do you see each other from time to time?"*
—Nos vemos todos los días.	*"We see each other every day."*
Hugo y Virginia se querían mucho.	*Hugo and Virginia loved each other a lot.*

H. Mejores amigos. Describe the relationship between best friends. Complete each sentence with the verb in parentheses and the reflexive pronoun that shows reciprocal action.

Modelos   Rita y Lucía <u>se llaman</u> todos los días. (llamar)

           Rita y yo <u>nos llamamos</u> todos los días. (llamar)

1. Fernando y Fernanda _____ por teléfono muchas veces al día. (hablar)

2. Gabriela y yo _____ con la tarea. (ayudar)

3. Víctor y yo _____ mensajes por correo electrónico. (mandar)

4. María y Paco _____ durante las vacaciones. (escribir)

5. Alicia y Diego _____ muy bien. (comprender)

6. Cuando Nati y yo _____, _____ un abrazo. (ver / dar)

7. Marcos y Emilia _____ mucho. (querer)

8. Rómulo y Carmen _____ muy bien. (conocer)

III. The Impersonal Use of *se*

- In Spanish, the construction **se** + verb in the third-person singular or plural is used to avoid saying who performed the action of the verb. The verb agrees with the grammatical subject, which is usually the noun that follows the verb:

Se vende fruta.	*Fruit is sold. / They sell fruit.*
Se venden manzanas.	*Apples are sold. / They sell apples.*
Se habla español.	*Spanish is spoken. / We speak Spanish.*

- The verb is in the third-person singular when the subject is an infinitive:

Se prohibe sacar fotos.	*No taking photos. / Taking photos is prohibited.*

- The verb is always in the third-person singular for verbs that do not take a direct object (*intransitive verbs*):

Se vive bien en los Estados Unidos.	*People/We live well in the United States.*
Se entra/sale por aquí.	*You go in/out this way. (This is the way in/out.)*

- Reflexive verbs can only show an unidentified subject with the addition of **uno** or **una** to a third-person singular verb:

Uno se acuesta tarde los sábados.	*One goes/People go to bed late on Saturdays.*

I. **Petroteca, S.A.** *(Petroteca, Inc.)* To find out what's happening with this large corporation, write sentences using the impersonal **se** + verb in the third-person singular or third-person plural. Use the same tense as the original sentence.

Modelo   La compañía gana mucho dinero. ➤ Se gana mucho dinero.

1. Los jefes y los empleados trabajan mucho.

   _____

2. La empresa buscaba programadores.

   _____

3. Abrieron nuevas oficinas en Sudamérica.

   _____

4. Petroteca produce productos petroquímicos.

   _____

5. Instalaron un departamento de relaciones públicas.

   _____

6. Los fundadores fundaron la compañía en 1974.

   _____

7. Los ingenieros desarrollaban una nueva tecnología.

   _____

8. Petroteca, S.A. exporta a cien países.

   _____

IV. "To Become" in Spanish

- Different reflexive verbs are used in Spanish to express *become*. **Ponerse** + adjective is used commonly to express emotional or physical changes:

Lorenzo se puso furioso.	*Lorenzo became/got furious.*
Marta está poniéndose roja.	*Marta is blushing (getting red).*

- **Volverse** + adjective is used in the expression **volverse loco** *(to go crazy, mad):*

Creía que me iba a volver loco.	*I thought I was going to go crazy.*

- **Hacerse** and **llegar a ser** are used with nouns of profession or adjectives that show social status. Effort in becoming on the part of the subject is suggested:

Rafael se hizo/llegó a ser ingeniero. *Rafael became an engineer.*

Tú y yo nos hacemos/llegamos a ser amigos. *You and I are becoming friends.*

J. **¿Cómo se dice?** Complete each of the following sentences by selecting the correct expression for *become* and then writing the verbs in the preterit.

1. Roberto y Antonio _____ médicos.

2. Esos chicos acatarrados _____ muy pálidos.

3. Nosotros _____ ricos como directores de la empresa.

4. Amparo _____ loca por sus problemas.

5. Yo _____ muy contenta al recibir los regalos.

6. ¿Cuándo _____ tú programadora?

K. **Preguntas personales.** Answer the following questions in complete Spanish sentences.

1. ¿A qué hora te despiertas/te acuestas todos los días?

_____

2. ¿Qué ropa te pusiste hoy?

_____

3. ¿Te rompiste el brazo, la mano o la pierna alguna vez? ¿Qué pasó?

_____

4. ¿Te pusiste rojo/roja alguna vez? ¿Por qué?

_____

5. ¿Te enojas o te ofendes fácilmente? ¿Qué cosas te enojan o te ofenden?

_____

6. ¿Quién es tu mejor amigo/amiga? ¿Cuándo se conocieron? ¿Cuándo se ven?

_____

➤➤➤➤➤

7. ¿Qué se vende en las tiendas donde vives?

_____

8. ¿Qué cosas se hacen en casa/en el centro/en el campo?

_____

_____

L. Composición. Write eight sentences describing the things you did today and where, when, or with whom you did them. Use reflexive verbs of personal hygiene and emotions, as well as others such as **irse, reunirse (con), acordarse (de), olvidarse (de).** Also use reciprocal reflexives and the impersonal **se** as needed.

The Present Perfect; The Past Perfect; Past Participles as Adjectives

I. The Present Perfect Tense

■ The present perfect tense is a *compound tense,* which means that it is made up of two parts: a conjugated form of the present tense of **haber** + a past participle. In this role, **haber** is called an *auxiliary,* or helping, *verb.*

■ The past participle is the form of the verb that ends in **-do.** The past participle of regular verbs is formed by dropping the infinitive ending and adding **-ado** to the stem of **-ar** verbs and **-ido** to the stem of **-er** and **-ir** verbs. When it is used in the present perfect tense, the past participle does not change to show number or gender.

■ The present perfect in Spanish, like the equivalent tense in English, describes past events that continue into or have an effect on the present. Study the conjugation of the present perfect tense of **llegar:**

yo **he llegado**	nosotros/nosotras **hemos llegado**
tú **has llegado**	vosotros/vosotras **habéis llegado**
él ella } **ha llegado** Ud.	ellos ellas } **han llegado** Uds.

No hemos salido todavía.   *We haven't left yet.*

Ya han llegado.   *They have already arrived.*

■ The following verbs have irregular past participles:

abrir ➤ **abierto**	morir ➤ **muerto**
cubrir ➤ **cubierto**	poner ➤ **puesto**
decir ➤ **dicho**	romper ➤ **roto**
escribir ➤ **escrito**	ver ➤ **visto**
freír ➤ **frito**	volver ➤ **vuelto**
hacer ➤ **hecho**	

Note: When a prefix is added to these verbs, the past participle continues to be irregular: **describir** ➤ *descrito (described),* **descubrir** ➤ *descubierto (discovered),* **devolver** ➤ *devuelto (returned).*

■ The participles of **-er** and **-ir** verbs whose stems end in a vowel not preceded by a **-u-** have an accent mark over the **-i-** in the past participle:

caer ➤ **caído**	traer ➤ **traído**
creer ➤ **creído**	construir ➤ **construido**
leer ➤ **leído**	destruir ➤ **destruido**
oír ➤ **oído**	huir ➤ **huido**

- In the present perfect tense, object pronouns precede the forms of **haber.** They cannot be attached to the past participle. In questions, subject pronouns must follow the past participle. They can never be placed between the auxiliary verbs and the past participle:

Se lo hemos dicho.	*We've said it to him.*
No me he bañado todavía.	*I haven't taken a bath yet.*
¿Por qué no nos ha llamado Ud.?	*Why haven't you called us?*
¿Qué han hecho Uds.?	*What have you done?*

Note: See Chapter 11 to review direct and indirect object pronouns, and see Chapter 16 for reflexive verbs.

A. Recién llegadas en Salamanca *(Recently arrived in Salamanca).* Cecilia and Daniela have gone to Salamanca, Spain, to study Spanish for the summer. Write the correct forms of the verbs in the present perfect tense to find out what Cecilia has written to their parents. (Note: The reflexive and object pronouns are already in place.)

Para poner al día (To bring up to date)

a propósito *by the way*	**ocurrírsele a uno** *to occur to someone*
instalarse *to get settled in*	**salírsele un novio** *to get a boyfriend*
matricularse *to get enrolled*	**los trámites** *procedures*

Queridos papás:

¿Cómo _____ (1. estar) Uds.? Daniela y yo nos

_____ (2. instalar). Los directores de la escuela de verano

nos _____ (3. dar) un cuarto muy grande en la residencia y

nos _____ (4. ayudar) mucho con los trámites. Daniela

y yo nos _____ (5. matricularse) en la universidad

y las clases ya _____ (6. empezar). (Nosotras)

_____ (7. conocer) a muchos estudiantes de otros países.

(Nosotras) _____ (8. ir) de excursión con unos chicos muy

simpáticos. Ya (nosotras) _____ (9. hacer) muchas cosas.

(Nosotras) _____ (10. ver) el Patio de las Escuelas, las

Catedrales y la Plaza Mayor. ¡Nos _____ (11. impresionar)

todo! No se preocupen. Hasta ahora, nosotras _____

(12. comer) muy bien. Ah, a propósito, se me _____

(13. ocurrir) otra cosa. Todavía (yo) no les _____ (14. decir)

esto. ¡A Daniela se le _____ (15. salir) un novio!

¡Uno de esos chicos ingleses! Un abrazo muy fuerte de Cecilia.

Salamanca

- The city of **Salamanca** lies northwest of Madrid in the regional government (**comunidad autónoma**) of Castilla-León. Salamanca was and remains a great center of learning and a vibrant university city full of history and character. The University of Salamanca, founded in 1215, became an important, prestigious institution supported by kings and Popes. Its fame spread, and by the sixteenth century, it had 70 professors and 12,000 students. Among its famous alumni and professors were Fray Luis de León and San Juan de la Cruz, sixteenth-century theologians and writers, and Miguel de Unamuno (1864–1936), the celebrated writer and philosopher.

- The historical center of the city is picturesque. **El Patio de las Escuelas** is a square famous for its sixteenth-century Renaissance buildings and design. The facade of the university buildings, dating from 1534, is so finely sculpted that it looks like a silversmith's work, an example of the Plateresque style (**estilo plateresco**). There is a bronze statue of Fray Luis de León in the center of the patio, and the hall where he lectured in theology retains the furnishings of the period. Fray Luis is buried in the chapel.

- **La Catedral nueva** was built between 1513 and 1560, but it received additions until the eighteenth century. As a result, it is an impressive combination of the Gothic (**gótico**), Renaissance (**renacentista**), and Baroque (**barroco**) styles. **La Catedral vieja** is a beautiful Romanesque (**románico**) building from the twelfth century. **La Plaza Mayor,** one of the most beautiful squares in Spain, was built for the city by Felipe V (1683–1746), the first Bourbon king of Spain. It was Felipe V who established the **Real Academia Española de la Lengua** in 1714, patterned after the French Academy.

B. Quehaceres domésticos. The twins Alejo and Nieves are told to help around the house with some chores. Write sentences with verbs in the present perfect to say that they've already done these things. Change direct object nouns to pronouns and make all necessary changes.

Modelo   —Nieves, hija, haz la cama.
    ➤ —Ya la he hecho, mamá.

Palabras útiles

colgar (o ➤ ue) *to hang*

regar (e ➤ ie) *to water*

---

1. —Alejo, hijo, corta el césped.

   — _____

2. —Alejo y Nieves, hijos, pongan el garaje en orden.

   — _____

3. —Nieves, hija, riega las flores.

   — _____

4. —Nieves y Alejo, hijos, sacudan el polvo en la sala.

   — _____

5. —Nieves, hija, pasa la aspiradora.

   — _____

6. —Alejo, hijo, recoge los periódicos.

   — _____

7. —Alejo y Nieves, hijos, cuelguen los cuadros en el comedor.

   — _____

C. Pero antes de salir... People say that they are ready to go out because they've already done the things asked about. Answer the questions in the present perfect tense. Change direct object nouns to pronouns and make all necessary changes.

Modelo   —Vas a ducharte, ¿no?
    ➢ —Me he duchado ya.

1. —Uds. van a vestirse, ¿no?

   —_____

2. —Consuelo va a lavarse el pelo, ¿no?

   —_____

3. —Vas a ponerte los zapatos, ¿no?

   —_____

4. —Ana María y Esteban van a darle agua al perro, ¿no?

   —_____

5. —Ud. va a cepillarse el pelo, ¿no?

   —_____

6. —Jorge Luis va a afeitarse, ¿no?

   —_____

7. —Vais a llevarle el periódico a Federico, ¿no?

   —_____

II. The Past Perfect Tense

■ The past perfect (or pluperfect) tense is made up of the auxiliary verb **haber** in the imperfect tense + the past participle. It is the equivalent of *had done* something in English and marks an event that happened before another past event. Study the conjugation of **llegar** in the past perfect tense:

yo **había llegado**	nosotros/nosotras **habíamos llegado**
tú **habías llegado**	vosotros/vosotras **habíais llegado**
él ella } **había llegado** Ud.	ellos ellas } **habían llegado** Uds.

Ya **habían visto** la película.	*They had already seen the movie.*
Pili ya se **había desayunado** cuando su hermano se despertó.	*Pili had already had breakfast when her brother woke up.*

D. Demasiado tarde. Write sentences that explain what people had already done when other things happened. Use the past perfect tense to express what had already happened and the preterit to express what happened more recently.

Modelo   Laura / salir : Marta / llegar
➤ Laura había salido ya cuando Marta llegó.

1. yo / volver a casa : comenzar a llover

   _____

2. nosotros / acostarse : Paco / llamar a la puerta

   _____

3. tú / comer : tus amigos / invitarte a cenar

   _____

4. Uds. / irse : sonar / el teléfono

   _____

5. Miguel / hacer el proyecto : su jefe / darle otro

   _____

6. Felipe y Mirella / sacar entradas para el concierto : sus padres / regalarles unas

   _____

III. Past Participles as Adjectives

■ The past participle of most verbs can function as an adjective. It changes for number and gender like any other adjective with four forms:

La librería está *abierta* hasta las once.	*The bookstore is open until 11 o'clock.*
Me gustan los trajes *hechos* a la medida.	*I like tailor-made suits.*

E. **Los resultados.** Express the state these people are in as a result of having done or felt something. Write sentences with the verb **estar** and the correct form of the past participle.

Modelo Diana se ha preocupado. ➤ Está preocupada.

1. Tú *(masc.)* te has emocionado. _____

2. Ricardo y Silvia se han casado. _____

3. Ud. *(fem.)* se ha sentado. _____

4. Yo *(masc.)* me he vestido. _____

5. Uds. *(masc.)* se han relajado. _____

6. Las bisabuelas se han muerto. _____

7. Vosotros os habéis asustado. _____

8. Natalia se ha acostado. _____

F. **El participio pasado como adjetivo.** Complete each of the following sentences with the correct adjective (past participle) form of the verb in parentheses.

Frases útiles

a mano *by hand*

el asco *filthy, disgusting condition*

despedir *to fire*

freír *(past part. with* **estar***) to be washed up*

muy hecho *overcooked (meat)*

pasado *rotten, overripe (fruit)*

---

1. ¡Qué hermosas son esas montañas _____ de nieve! (cubrir)

2. No comas la carne. Está muy _____. (hacer)

3. Se puede reparar estos juguetes _____. (romper)

4. Estas blusas _____ a mano son preciosas. (hacer)

5. No me gustan las bananas tan _____. (pasar)

6. Hay que estudiar la lengua _____. (escribir)

7. ¿Cómo se ensuciaron estos niñitos? ¡Están _____ un asco! (hacer)

8. La mesa ya está _____. (poner)

9. El jefe despidió a Martín. ¡Martín está _____! (freír)

10. Voy a pie porque mi coche está _____. (descomponer)

G. **Preguntas personales.** Answer the following questions in complete Spanish sentences.

1. ¿Qué has hecho esta mañana antes de salir de la casa?

_____

2. ¿Con quiénes has hablado hoy?

_____

3. ¿Qué has escrito hoy?

_____

4. ¿Has hecho algo muy especial o interesante?

_____

5. ¿Te has preocupado o emocionado por algo recientemente?

_____

6. ¿Qué había pasado ya cuando llegaste a la clase de español hoy?

_____

7. ¿Prefieres la ropa hecha a mano o a máquina? ¿Por qué?

_____

H. **Composición.** Everyone is ready to spend a day in the country. Has everything been done in preparation for the picnic? Write eight to ten dialogue exchanges in which one person asks the other if something has been done, and the other person responds that it has or has not been done yet. For example:

    RITA: —¿Has hecho los sándwiches?
    PAULA: —Sí, los he hecho. (*or* Sí, están hechos.)

The Subjunctive: Present Tense; Uses of the Subjunctive

All the verb tenses presented thus far have been in the indicative mood. In this sense, *mood* refers to the general feeling or attitude. There is another mood in Spanish and English that is called the *subjunctive mood*. The indicative mood expresses events or states considered to be factual, definite, or part of the speaker's experience. The subjunctive mood expresses events or states considered not to be factual, definite, or part of the speaker's experience. For example, in the sentence *I wish that I were a millionaire, were* is in the subjunctive mood and expresses a state that is not factual. Although the subjunctive mood exists in both Spanish and English, it is used far more in Spanish.

I. The Subjunctive: Present Tense

Regular verbs

■ The present subjunctive is used in Spanish in subordinate (dependent) clauses after certain verbs and expressions. It is formed by changing the -a- in the present indicative endings to -e- for -**ar** verbs and the vowels -e- and -i- in the present indicative endings to -a- for -**er** and -**ir** verbs. The **yo** form ends in -**e** for -**ar** verbs and in -**a** for -**er** and -**ir** verbs. Study the following examples and note that the subject of the verb in the main clause *(quiere, esperan, prefieren)* differs from the subject in the subordinate (dependent) clause.

TRABAJAR

Quiere que *trabaje* el lunes.	*He wants me to work on Monday.*
Quiere que *trabajes* el lunes.	*He wants you to work on Monday.*
Quiere que *trabaje* el lunes.	*He wants her to work on Monday.*
Quiere que *trabajemos* el lunes.	*He wants us to work on Monday.*
Quiere que *trabajéis* el lunes.	*He wants you to work on Monday.*
Quiere que *trabajen* el lunes.	*He wants them to work on Monday.*

APRENDER

Esperan que *aprenda* español.	*They hope I'll learn Spanish.*
Esperan que *aprendas* español.	*They hope you'll learn Spanish.*
Esperan que *aprenda* español.	*They hope he'll learn Spanish.*
Esperan que *aprendamos* español.	*They hope we'll learn Spanish.*
Esperan que *aprendáis* español.	*They hope you'll learn Spanish.*
Esperan que *aprendan* español.	*They hope they'll learn Spanish.*

ABRIR

Prefieren que *abra* el paquete.	*They prefer that I open the package.*
Prefieren que *abras* el paquete.	*They prefer that you open the package.*
Prefieren que *abra* el paquete.	*They prefer that she open the package.*
Prefieren que *abramos* el paquete.	*They prefer that we open the package.*
Prefieren que *abráis* el paquete.	*They prefer that you open the package.*
Prefieren que *abran* el paquete.	*They prefer that they open the package.*

Stem-changing verbs

■ **-Ar** and **-er** verbs that have changes in the vowel of the stem in the present indicative have the same changes in the present subjunctive:

Desean que *te despiertes* temprano.   *They want you to wake up early.*
Desean que *nos despertemos*   *They want us to wake up early.*
   temprano.

¿Insiste en que él *vuelva* hoy?   *Do you insist that he return today?*
¿Insiste en que *volvamos* hoy?   *Do you insist that we return today?*

■ **-Ir** verbs that have the change **e ➤ ie** or **e ➤ i** in the present indicative also have these changes in the present subjunctive. These verbs also have **-i-** in the stem of the **nosotros** and **vosotros** forms in the present subjunctive. **Dormir** and **morir** have the **o ➤ ue** change in the present subjunctive and **u** in the stem of the **nosotros** and **vosotros** forms:

SENTIR

sienta	sintamos	
sientas	sintáis	
sienta	sientan	

SERVIR

sirva	sirvamos
sirvas	sirváis
sirva	sirvan

DORMIR

duerma	durmamos
duermas	durmáis
duerma	duerman

A. Quieren que... People want certain things to happen. Write sentences about what they want, prefer, and hope to happen. Use the present indicative of **querer, preferir,** or **esperar** in the main clause and the present subjunctive of the verb given in the sentence in the dependent clause. Link the two clauses with **que.**

Modelo   Mis amigos me llaman. : yo / querer
          ➤ Quiero que mis amigos me llamen.

1. Verónica y David regresan el miércoles. : nosotros / esperar

   _____

2. Yo leo *El País.* : Ud. / preferir

   _____

3. Uds. compran el periódico *ABC.* : yo / querer

   _____

4. Escuchas las noticias en la radio. : Roberto / preferir

   _____

5. Te interesan los programas de televisión. : nosotras / esperar

   _____

6. ¿Discutimos unos temas políticos? : tú / querer

   _____

7. Uds. me venden su coche. : yo / esperar

   _____

8. Anita asiste al concierto. : Uds. / querer

   _____

9. ¿Nos desayunamos a las nueve? : vosotras / preferir

   _____

10. Recibimos el paquete mañana. : tú / esperar

    _____

11. Ellos sirven platos peruanos. : Maricarmen / querer

    _____

12. Tú no duermes hasta las once. : tus padres / preferir

    _____

España: La democracia y los medios de comunicación

- Spain's three years of bloody civil war (1936–1939) ended with the defeat of the Republicans by General Francisco Franco and the Nationalist forces. Franco established a dictatorship that enforced rigorous censorship. The government controlled the media, and the press could print nothing that was unfavorable to the government. In 1969, Franco named Prince Juan Carlos de Borbón, the grandson of King Alfonso XIII, to succeed him upon his death. Juan Carlos ascended to the throne in 1975, announcing his plans for reform and his intention of making Spain a democracy. Spain is now a pluralist parliamentary democracy in which its citizens are guaranteed their political freedoms. The country's transformation from an authoritarian, highly centralized government into a democracy without civil war and bloodshed is one of the great events of the twentieth century.

- After Franco's death, there was a surge in newspaper and magazine publishing. But Spaniards did not trust newspapers and had lost the habit of reading them during the many years of repression. In addition, they were accustomed to getting their news from television and radio. Today, however, there are several important newspapers published in Spain. Perhaps the most influential is *El País*, which was founded in 1976 and was responsible for guiding the formation of opinion in the early years of democracy. The newspaper's slant is fairly liberal. The newspaper *ABC*, founded in 1905, had a conservative-monarchist viewpoint and was very popular during Franco's regime. Its readership declined after 1975. Other major dailies are *La Vanguardia*, a conservative Barcelona newspaper founded in 1881; *Diario 16*, which began to publish in 1975, three years after the weekly *Cambio 16*; and *Marca*, a daily devoted exclusively to sports, which began publishing in 1940. *Marca* was particularly popular during the Franco regime because it provided the only uncensored news.

Irregular verbs

- Verbs that have an irregularity in the **yo** form of the present indicative have the same irregularity in all forms of the present subjunctive. Only -**er** and -**ir** verbs have the -**g**- in the **yo** form, so all the present subjunctive endings have the vowel -**a**-. Study the following chart:

infinitive	present indicative (*yo* form)	present subjunctive
caer	caigo	**caiga, caigas, caiga, caigamos, caigáis, caigan**
decir	digo	**diga, digas, diga, digamos, digáis, digan**
hacer	hago	**haga, hagas, haga, hagamos, hagáis, hagan**
oír	oigo	**oiga, oigas, oiga, oigamos, oigáis, oigan**
poner	pongo	**ponga, pongas, ponga, pongamos, pongáis, pongan**
salir	salgo	**salga, salgas, salga, salgamos, salgáis, salgan**
tener	tengo	**tenga, tengas, tenga, tengamos, tengáis, tengan**

traer	traigo	**traiga, traigas, traiga, traigamos, traigáis, traigan**
venir	vengo	**venga, vengas, venga, vengamos, vengáis, vengan**

■ The following verbs also are irregular in the **yo** form:

infinitive	present indicative (*yo* form)	present subjunctive
caber	quepo	**quepa, quepas, quepa, quepamos, quepáis, quepan**
conocer	conozco	**conozca, conozcas, conozca, conozcamos, conozcáis, conozcan**
nacer	nazco	**nazca, nazcas, nazca, nazcamos, nazcáis, nazcan**
parecer	parezco	**parezca, parezcas, parezca, parezcamos, parezcáis, parezcan**
construir	construyo	**construya, construyas, construya, construyamos, construyáis, construyan**
destruir	destruyo	**destruya, destruyas, destruya, destruyamos, destruyáis, destruyan**
ver	veo	**vea, veas, vea, veamos, veáis, vean**

■ **Dar** and **estar** are regular in the present subjunctive except for the accent marks:

DAR		ESTAR	
dé	demos	esté	estemos
des	deis	estés	estéis
dé	den	esté	estén

■ **Ser, ir, saber,** and **haber** have irregular stems and regular endings in the present subjunctive:

infinitive	subjunctive stem	present subjunctive
ser	se-	**sea, seas, sea, seamos, seáis, sean**
ir	vay-	**vaya, vayas, vaya, vayamos, vayáis, vayan**
saber	sep-	**sepa, sepas, sepa, sepamos, sepáis, sepan**
haber	hay-	**haya, hayas, haya, hayamos, hayáis, hayan**

Note: Hay in the present subjunctive is **haya.**

B. **Nuestra familia.** The members of the Sánchez family express their feelings about each other. Write sentences using the present subjunctive to find out what they think. (Don't forget to use **que** to join the present indicative clause with the subjunctive clause.)

Modelo la señora Sánchez / querer : nosotros / conocer a su familia
➤ La señora Sánchez quiere que conozcamos a su familia.

1. los abuelos / alegrarse de : sus nietos / venir a verlos

2. todos / insistir en : haber / reunión familiar

_____

3. la madre / querer : sus hijos / hacer planes

_____

4. Pedro / sentir : sus hermanos / no verse mucho

_____

5. tú / esperar : todos / ser felices

_____

6. el padre / necesitar : Esteban / ir a trabajar con él

_____

7. nosotros / desear : María Elena / tener novio

_____

8. Leonora / preferir : tú / salir con Nacho

_____

Verbs with spelling changes

■ -**Ar** verbs whose stem ends in -**c, -g,** or -**z** make the following changes in all forms of the present subjunctive: **c ➤ qu, g ➤ gu, z ➤ c:**

Tocas la flauta. ➤ **Prefiero que** _toques_ **la flauta.**

Llegamos el sábado. ➤ **Esperan que** _lleguemos_ **el sábado.**

Se tranquilizan. ➤ **Es necesario que** _se tranquilicen._

■ -**Er** and -**ir** verbs whose stems end in -**c, -g,** or -**gu** make the following changes in all forms of the present subjunctive: **c ➤ z, g ➤ j, gu ➤ g:**

Te convencen. ➤ **Esperamos que** _te convenzan._

Escoges unas revistas. ➤ **Prefieren que** _escojas_ **unas revistas.**

Siguen los consejos. ➤ **Quiero que** _sigan_ **los consejos.**

■ Verbs that end in **-iar** or **-uar** and have an accent mark on the **i** or the **u** in the singular and third-person plural forms of the present indicative have the accent mark in the corresponding forms of the present subjunctive:

ENVIAR

envíe	enviemos
envíes	enviéis
envíe	envíen

CONTINUAR

continúe	continuemos
continúes	continuéis
continúe	continúen

C. Un concierto. Explain what the conductor, the musicians, and the audience want to happen. Answer the questions by writing sentences in the present subjunctive. Use the cues in parentheses to create your sentences. Pay particular attention to spelling changes in the subjunctive forms.

Modelo ¿Qué quiere el público? (el director y los músicos / trabajar bien juntos)
➤ Quiere que el director y los músicos trabajen bien juntos.

1. ¿Qué espera el director de orquesta? (los músicos / tranquilizarse)

   _____

2. ¿Qué siente el director? (los músicos / no llegar temprano)

   _____

3. ¿Qué quiere el director? (nosotros / empezar a tocar)

   _____

4. ¿Qué es necesario? (el público / sacar entradas pronto)

   _____

5. ¿En qué insiste el director? (los violines / seguirlo atentamente)

   _____

6. ¿Qué queremos? (el director / dirigir bien)

   _____

7. ¿Qué esperas? (la orquesta / tocar una sinfonía de Brahms)

   _____

8. ¿Qué desea el público? (el concierto / comenzar a las ocho en punto)

   _____

➤➤➤➤➤

9. ¿Qué espera la pianista? (su secretaria / enviarle la música)

   _____

10. ¿Qué quiere el público? (el espectáculo / continuar)

   _____

II. Uses of the Subjunctive

The subjunctive in noun clauses

- A *noun clause* is a clause that functions as a noun and can serve as either the subject or the object of a verb. Noun clauses that are part of a longer sentence are called *dependent* or *subordinate clauses*. They are introduced by the conjunction **que:**

  Oigo que *Pedro está de vuelta.*   *I hear (that) Pedro is back.*

  In this example, **Oigo** is the independent, or main, clause; **que Pedro está de vuelta** is the dependent (subordinate) clause. Note that in Spanish, **que** always introduces the dependent clause, but in English, *that* is often omitted before a dependent clause.

- The present subjunctive in Spanish is used in dependent (subordinate) noun clauses that follow main clauses that express the following:

1. *Imposition of will.* The subjunctive is used when the subject wants, needs, prefers, suggests, or insists that someone do something. The following verbs and impersonal expressions in the main clause require the subjunctive in the dependent clause:

verbs	impersonal expressions
desear *to wish*	**es importante que** *it's important that*
insistir en *to insist on*	**es mejor que** *it's better that*
necesitar *to need*	**es necesario que** *it's necessary that*
preferir (e ➤ ie) *to prefer*	**es preciso que** *it's necessary that*
querer (e ➤ ie) *to want*	**ojalá que** *I hope that; let's hope that; here's hoping that*
recomendar (e ➤ ie) *to recommend*	
sugerir (e ➤ ie) *to suggest*	

Study the following examples:

Quiero que Uds. se queden.	*I want you to stay.*
Necesitamos que lo hagas.	*We need you to do it.*
Insisten en que yo diga que sí.	*They insist that I say yes.*
Prefiere que almorcemos ahora.	*He prefers that we have lunch now.*
Es necesario que estudies más.	*It's necessary that you study more.*
Es importante que comamos bien.	*It's important that we eat well.*
Ojalá que vayas con nosotros.	*I hope (that) you'll go with us.*

2. *Emotions and attitudes.* The subjunctive is used after verbs and impersonal expressions that express the speaker's emotional reaction to or evaluation of the action of the subjordinate clause. Among the verbs and impersonal expressions that convey emotion and attitude are the following:

verbs	impersonal expressions
alegrarse (de) *to be glad, happy*	**es bueno que** *it's good that*
extrañar *to be surprised*	**es imposible que** *it's impossible that*
gustar *to like*	**es posible que** *it's possible that*
sentir (e > ie) *to regret, be sorry*	**es una lástima que** *it's a pity/shame that*
sorprender *to surprise*	
temer *to fear*	
tener miedo (de) *to fear, be afraid*	

Note that **extrañar, sorprender,** and **gustar** are used with an indirect object pronoun. Study the following examples:

Me alegro de que todos estén bien.	*I'm glad (that) everyone is well.*
Siento que Paco esté enfermo.	*I'm sorry (that) Paco is ill.*
Les extraña que no lo sepamos.	*They're surprised (that) we don't know it.*
Tenemos miedo de que se haga daño.	*We're afraid she'll hurt herself.*
Le gusta que ayudes.	*He likes you to help.*
Es posible que vuelva hoy.	*It's possible (that) she'll return today.*
Es bueno que lo pasen tan bien.	*It's good (that) you're having such a good time.*
Es una lástima que tengan problemas.	*It's a pity (that) they have problems.*

3. *Doubt and uncertainty.* The impersonal expressions **es cierto** and **es verdad** are followed by the indicative, but when they are negative, **no es cierto** and **no es verdad,** they are followed by the subjunctive. Similarly, the verbs **creer** and **pensar** used in the negative require the subjunctive in the dependent clause:

Creo/Pienso que está en la Florida.	*I think he's in Florida.*
No creo/No pienso que esté **en la Florida.**	*I don't think he's in Florida.*

The verb **dudar** *(to doubt)* requires the subjunctive in the dependent clause. But when **dudar** is used in the negative, the verb in the dependent clause is in the indicative:

Dudamos **que** *llueva* **por la tarde.**	*We doubt it will rain in the afternoon.*
No dudamos que llueve por la tarde.	*We don't doubt it will rain in the afternoon.*

- If the subject of the main clause and the dependent clause is the same, the verb in the main clause is used with an infinitive: **Prefiero *viajar* en tren** *(I prefer to travel by train)*. However, if the subject of the main clause is different from the subject in the dependent clause, the verb in the dependent clause is in the subjunctive: **Prefiero que *viajen* en tren** *(I prefer they travel by train)*.

D. Es importante que sepan el subjuntivo. Use the cues to write sentences with the subjunctive in the dependent clause. Then identify the use of the subjunctive in the sentence.

Modelo   los Gómez / insistir en : sus hijos / ponerse las botas
  ➤ Los Gómez insisten en que sus hijos se pongan las botas.
    Uso: *Imposition of will*

1. tú / dudar : Ignacio / irse mañana

   _____

   Uso: _____

2. es mejor : Uds. / no jugar en el parque ahora

   _____

   Uso: _____

3. es bueno : nosotros / tener tantos amigos

   _____

   Uso: _____

4. yo / extrañar : la profesora / saber bailar el tango

   _____

   Uso: _____

5. el psicólogo / recomendar : todos / expresar los sentimientos

   _____

   Uso: _____

6. Lidia e Iris / no creer : los Cachorros / ganar la Serie Mundial de béisbol

   _____

   Uso: _____

E. **¿Subjuntivo, indicativo o infinitivo?** Write the present subjunctive, the present indicative, or the infinitive of the verb in parentheses to complete each of the following sentences.

1. Es necesario que Uds. _____ ahora mismo. (vestirse)

2. Creo que Alejo _____ razón. (tener)

3. Dudamos que ellos _____ la película esta semana. (dar)

4. Maximiliano y José quieren _____ en forma. (ponerse)

5. Es posible que esos chicos no _____ muy responsables. (ser)

6. Ojalá que Jorge nos _____ lo que pasó en la reunión. (decir)

7. Raimundo piensa _____ este año. (graduarse)

8. Me extraña que Julia no _____ usar la computadora. (saber)

9. Oigo que vosotros _____ pronto. (irse)

10. Es una lástima que yo no _____ verte. (conseguir)

11. No creen que Sara _____ acompañarlos. (poder)

12. Es importante que Uds. _____ nuestros consejos. (seguir)

13. Chelo tiene miedo de que no _____ entradas. (quedar)

14. Esperamos que no _____ muchas dificultades. (haber)

15. Es mejor que tú _____ la televisión. (apagar)

16. No dudo que Uds. _____ a mis hermanos. (conocer)

17. Pienso que los Fernández _____ casa. (buscar)

18. La señora Iriarte sugiere que nosotros _____ español.
(practicar)

F. **Me gusta que...** Everyone has opinions about the weather. Tell what these people think by rewriting each sentence using the verb or phrase in parentheses and the present subjunctive or the present indicative of the verb.

Modelo   Hace buen tiempo. (Me gusta)
➤ Me gusta que haga buen tiempo.

1. Hace sol. (Nos alegramos de)

_____

2. Empieza a nevar. (Vemos)

_____

➤➤➤➤➤

3. Está lloviendo. (¡Qué lástima!)

_____

4. Va a hacer mucho frío. (Sienten)

_____

5. Está nublado. (Me parece)

_____

6. Nieva hoy. (No pienso)

_____

7. Llueve a cántaros. (¿No oyes?)

_____

G. Reacciones. Two people react differently when you give them a piece of news: one simply acknowledges the news while the other expresses an opinion. Tell what they say by writing sentences using the verbs or phrases in parentheses and the present subjunctive or the present indicative of the verb.

Modelo   —Clara sale con Paco. (Prefiero / Veo)
   ➤ —Prefiero que Clara salga con Paco.
   ➤ —Veo que Clara sale con Paco.

1. —Olga rompe con su novio. (Es cierto / Es probable)

— _____

— _____

2. —Jacinto estudia para ingeniero. (Espero / Dicen)

— _____

— _____

3. —Marisol sigue las costumbres de su familia. (Es verdad / Me gusta)

— _____

— _____

4. —Alano y Patricia se casan. (No dudamos / Nos sorprende)

— _____

— _____

5. —La empresa es muy próspera. (Ojalá / Sé)

— _____

— _____

H. **Preguntas personales.** Answer the following questions in complete Spanish sentences. Use the present subjunctive wherever possible.

1. ¿Es importante/necesario que hagas ciertas cosas? ¿Cuáles son?

_____

2. ¿Es bueno que haya muchos cambios en la vida/la sociedad/el mundo? ¿Por qué?

_____

3. ¿Qué esperas que pase durante el año próximo?

_____

4. ¿De qué te alegras? ¿Qué sientes?

_____

5. ¿Qué piensas regalarles a tus padres/tus hermanos/tus amigos?

_____

6. ¿Qué esperas que te regalen a ti?

_____

I. **Composición.** What are some wishes for other people that you hope will come true? Write a list of ten hopes, wishes, or dreams. Begin each sentence with a verb or an expression that will require the present subjunctive in the dependent clause: **Espero que..., Quiero/Deseo que..., Ojalá que..., Es posible que....**

The Future Tense;
The Conditional Tense

I. The Future Tense

■ The future tense in Spanish is formed by adding a special set of endings to the infinitive. These endings are the same for -**ar,** -**er,** and -**ir** verbs:

ESTUDIAR

yo estudiar**é**	nosotros/nosotras estudiar**emos**
tú estudiar**ás**	vosotros/vosotras estudiar**éis**
él ⎤	ellos ⎤
ella ⎬ estudiar**á**	ellas ⎬ estudiar**án**
Ud. ⎦	Uds. ⎦

LEER

yo leer**é**	nosotros/nosotras leer**emos**
tú leer**ás**	vosotros/vosotras leer**éis**
él ⎤	ellos ⎤
ella ⎬ leer**á**	ellas ⎬ leer**án**
Ud. ⎦	Uds. ⎦

VIVIR

yo vivir**é**	nosotros/nosotras vivir**emos**
tú vivir**ás**	vosotros/vosotras vivir**éis**
él ⎤	ellos ⎤
ella ⎬ vivir**á**	ellas ⎬ vivir**án**
Ud. ⎦	Uds. ⎦

■ For some verbs, the future-tense endings are added to modified forms of the infinitive:

caber ➢ **cabré**	poder ➢ **podré**	salir ➢ **saldré**
decir ➢ **diré**	poner ➢ **pondré**	tener ➢ **tendré**
haber ➢ **habré**	querer ➢ **querré**	valer ➢ **valdré**
hacer ➢ **haré**	saber ➢ **sabré**	venir ➢ **vendré**

Note: Hay in the future tense is **habrá.**

■ In the future tense, -**ir** verbs that have an accent mark in the infinitive lose the accent mark in the future: **oír** ➢ *oiré,* **reír** ➢ *reiré.*

■ The future tense in Spanish is often replaced by the **ir a** + infinitive construction. This construction, however, refers to the immediate future, whereas the future tense refers to the remote future, as well as the immediate future:

Haremos un viaje en julio.	*We'll take a trip in July.*
Vamos a hacer un viaje en julio.	*We're going to take a trip in July.*

A. Nuestros planes. Tell what you and your friends will do on the weekend. Rewrite each of the following sentences by changing the verb from the present tense to the future tense.

Modelo Nora visita a sus abuelos.
➤ Nora visitará a sus abuelos.

1. Lupe y yo vamos al museo.

Lupe y yo iremos al museo

2. Ves la nueva película inglesa.

verá la nueva película inglesa

3. Ud. descansa.

descansará

4. Pablo y Leonora salen a una discoteca.

Pablo y Leonora saldrán a una discoteca

5. Griselda corre cinco millas.

Griselda correrá cinco millas

6. Uds. asisten a un concierto.

Uds. asistirán a un concierto

7. Hago una excursión.

Haré una excursión

8. Venís a vernos.

Vendrás a vernos

B. ¿Qué querrán hacer? What will you and your out-of-town relatives do when they come to visit you? Write sentences with verbs in the future tense.

Modelo Rafael / conocer la ciudad ➤ Rafael conocerá la ciudad.

1. mis primos / querer ver un partido de baloncesto

Mis primos querrán ver un partido de baloncesto

2. yo / poder llevar a mis parientes al museo

Yo podré llevar a mis parientes al museo

➤➤➤➤➤

3. tú / tener que acompañar a las primas al almacén

Tú tendrás que acompañar a las primas al almacén

4. nosotros / enseñarles la escuela

Nosotros enseñaremosles la escuela

5. la abuela / venir a vernos

La abuela vendrá a vernos

6. Uds. / salir al teatro

Uds. saldrán al teatro

7. Ud. / comer algo en un café

Ud. comerá algo en un café

8. vosotros / hacer turismo

Vosotros haremos turismo

C. Después de graduarse. Tell what plans people have after they graduate.
Rewrite each of the following sentences. Remove the conjugated verb in the
verb + (word) + infinitive construction. Then write the remaining infinitive
in the future tense.

Modelo Ud. espera tocar trompeta en una banda.
➤ Ud. tocará trompeta en una banda.

1. Mateo piensa seguir estudiando.

Mateo seguirá estudiando

2. Tú tienes que trabajar con tu padre.

Tú trabajarás con tu padre

3. Ud. debe mudarse a su propio apartamento.

Ud. deberá mudarse a su propio apartamento

4. Laura y yo vamos a hacer un viaje a Oaxaca.

Laura y yo iremos a hacer un viaje a Oaxaca

5. Yo quiero vivir en el centro.

Yo querré vivir en el centro

6. Pedro y Jaime van a comprar un coche.

Pedro y Jaime irán a comprar un coche

7. Uds. piensan viajar a Guadalajara.

Uds. pensáran viajar a Guadalajara

8. Vosotros vais a tener muchos planes.

Vosotros iréis a tener muchos planes

México

■ **Oaxaca,** Mexico's fifth largest state, is in the south of Mexico. It is known for its beautiful beaches on the Pacific Ocean, as well as for the Sierra Madre mountains, forests, plains, and valleys. Oaxaca is an important archaeological center of pre-Columbian indigenous cultures. **Monte Albán,** the ancient capital of the Zapotecs, attracts thousands of tourists each year. Indian traditions, festivals, and crafts abound throughout the state of Oaxaca and its capital city of the same name.

■ **Guadalajara** is Mexico's second largest city in population. It is the capital of the state of Jalisco, which lies northwest of Mexico City on the Pacific Ocean. Guadalajara is an appealing city because of its sophisticated European atmosphere and colonial architecture. The historical center of the city is the **Plaza de Armas** with its cathedral, constructed between 1561 and 1618, and the **Palacio de Gobierno** (1643), where some Orozco murals can be seen. Visitors enjoy the parks, markets, and folkloric features of Guadalajara, such as mariachi music and the popular dance **el jarabe tapatío.** The inhabitants of Guadalajara are called **tapatíos.**

D. ¿Qué serás? Tell what profession you and your friends will have by writing sentences with the verb **ser** in the future tense. (Be sure that the profession agrees with the subject.)

Modelo   Ana y Carlos / médico ➤ Serán médicos.

1. tú (*fem.*) / abogado   _Serás abogada_

2. nosotros / programador   _Seremos programador_

3. yo (*masc.*) / ingeniero   _Seré ingeniero_

4. Ud. (*masc.*) / dentista   _será dentisto_

5. Rebeca / arquitecto   _será arquitecta_

6. Uds. (*fem.*) / profesor   _serán profesoras_

7. Teresa y Samuel / escritor   _serán escritores_

8. vosotros / cocinero   _seréis cocineros_

E. **¡Qué día!** You and the members of your family have a very busy day tomorrow, so everyone must get an early start. Tell what people must do by writing the verbs in parentheses in the future tense.

Mañana mis padres, mis hermanos y yo ___*tendremos*___

(1. tener) que salir de la casa muy temprano. Mis padres

___*se despertarán*___(2. despertarse) primero. Al levantarme,

yo ___*se limpiaré*___ (3. limpiarse) los dientes,

___*se ducharán*___ (4. ducharse) y ___*se vestirán*___

(5. vestirse) rápido. Mis hermanos ___*se lavarán*___ (6. lavarse)

y ___*se pensarán*___ (7. peinarse). Todos nosotros

___*se desayunaremos*___(8. desayunarse). Después, yo

___*se pondré*___ (9. ponerse) el abrigo y ___*saldré*___

(10. salir). ___*Habré*___ (11. Haber) mucho que hacer mañana.

¡Nosotros no ___*descansaremos*___(12. descansar) en todo el día!

12/12

- The future tense is commonly used in the main clause of a sentence that contains a dependent **si** clause (*if* clause) in the present tense. The order of the clauses can be reversed:

Si Elvira *almuerza,* **yo** *almorzaré* **también.**   *If Elvira has lunch, I'll have lunch too.*
Yo *almorzaré* **si Elvira** *almuerza.*   *I'll have lunch if Elvira has lunch.*

16/16

F. **Los estudios.** Complete the following two-clause sentences by writing the correct forms of the verbs in parentheses.

Modelo   Si Manolo ___estudia___ (estudiar) mucho, ___sacará___ (sacar) buenas notas.

1. Si los estudiantes ___*practican*___ (practicar) español,

   lo ___*perfeccionaré*___(perfeccionar).

2. Si Miguel ___*va*___ (ir) al laboratorio de lenguas,

   ___*podré*___ (poder) escuchar las cintas.

3. Tú ___*tienes*___ (tener) éxito si ___*haré*___ (hacer)

   toda la tarea.

4. Nosotros ___*sabemos*___ (saber) escribir mejor si

   ___*leeré*___ (leer) las obras clásicas.

5. Si Claudia y Hernán ___*estudian*___ (estudiar) mucho todos los

   días, ___*saldré*___ (salir) bien en los exámenes.

6. Yo ___quiero___ (querer) tomar dos clases adicionales

   si ___tendré___ (tener) tiempo.

7. Si la profesora me lo ___pide___ (pedir), yo

   ___pondré___ (poner) los ejercicios en la pizarra.

8. ¿Cuándo ___hace___ (hacer) vosotros las investigaciones

   si ___tendré___ (tener) que entregar el informe el viernes?

II. The Conditional Tense

- The Spanish conditional tense (expressed in English as *would* do something) is formed by adding the endings of the imperfect tense of -**er** and -**ir** verbs to the infinitive. These conditional endings are the same for -**ar**, -**er**, and -**ir** verbs:

VIAJAR

yo viajaría	nosotros/nosotras viajaríamos
tú viajarías	vosotros/vosotras viajaríais
él ⎱	ellos ⎱
ella ⎬ viajaría	ellas ⎬ viajarían
Ud. ⎰	Uds. ⎰

APRENDER

yo aprendería	nosotros/nosotras aprenderíamos
tú aprenderías	vosotros/vosotras aprenderíais
él ⎱	ellos ⎱
ella ⎬ aprendería	ellas ⎬ aprenderían
Ud. ⎰	Uds. ⎰

ESCRIBIR

yo escribiría	nosotros/nosotras escribiríamos
tú escribirías	vosotros/vosotras escribiríais
él ⎱	ellos ⎱
ella ⎬ escribiría	ellas ⎬ escribirían
Ud. ⎰	Uds. ⎰

Note: When *would* means *used to*, the imperfect tense is used:

Cuando vivíamos en el centro, íbamos a los museos a menudo.   *When we lived downtown, we would go to the museums often.*

- The verbs that have modified infinitives in the future tense have the same changes in the conditional tense:

caber ➤ **cabría**	poder ➤ **podría**	salir ➤ **saldría**
decir ➤ **diría**	poner ➤ **pondría**	tener ➤ **tendría**
haber ➤ **habría**	querer ➤ **querría**	valer ➤ **valdría**
hacer ➤ **haría**	saber ➤ **sabría**	venir ➤ **vendría**

Notes:

1. **Hay** in the conditional tense is **habría.**

2. When the main clause in Spanish has a verb of communication, knowledge, or belief (for example, **decir, saber,** or **creer**) in the present tense, the verb in the dependent (subordinate) clause is in the future tense. When the main clause has such a verb in one of the past tenses, the verb in the dependent clause is in the conditional tense:

Creo que se quedarán.	*I think they'll stay.*
Creía que *se quedarían.*	*I thought they would stay.*
Carmen dice que **saldrá.**	*Carmen says she'll go out.*
Carmen *dijo* que *saldría.*	*Carmen said she would go out.*

G. **¡Sería maravilloso!** What would Teo and his friends do with the money they won in the lottery? Write sentences in the conditional tense to find out.

Modelo Teo / comprarse un coche todo terreno
➤ Teo se compraría un coche todo terreno.

1. yo / hacer viajes

   Yo hacería viajes ~~Yo haría viajes~~

2. Íñigo y Felisa / seguir sus estudios universitarios

   Íñigo y Felisa seguirían sus estudios universitarios

3. Uds. / no preocuparse por nada

   Uds. nose preocuparían por nada

4. nosotros / jugar a la bolsa *(stock market)*

   Nosotros jugaríamos a la bolsa

5. Ud. / tener casa en todas las capitales del mundo

   Ud. tenería casa en todas las capitales del mundo

6. tú / dar dinero a las caridades *(charities)* importantes

   Tú darías dinero a las caridades importantes

7. vosotros / dejar de trabajar

   Vosotros dejaríais de trabajar

H. Me dedicaría a... *(I would spend my time . . .).* What would Catarina and her friends like to do in their spare time? Write sentences using the cue words to find out. All verbs should be in the conditional tense.

Modelo   (a Catarina) / gustar / leer libros de ciencia ficción
       ➤ Le gustaría leer libros de ciencia ficción.

1. (a mí) / encantar / dirigir una orquesta

    Me encantaría dirigir una orquesta

2. (Rubén y Rosario) / dedicarse a la pintura

    Le dedicarán a la pintura

3. (a nosotros) / interesar / hacer experimentos químicos

    interesaría
    Os interesaríamos hacer experimentos químicos

4. (tú) / ser director de cine

    serías director de cine

5. (Julián) / hacer alpinismo *(mountain climbing)*

    harías alpinismo

6. (Uds.) / gustar / decorar casas

    Les gustaría decorar casas

7. (vosotros) / jugar al béisbol en las ligas mayores

    jugaríais al béisbol en las ligas mayores

I. Preguntas personales. Answer the following questions in complete Spanish sentences.

1. ¿Cómo celebrarás tu cumpleaños? ¿Habrá fiesta?

    _____

2. ¿Qué harás este fin de semana?

    _____

3. ¿Qué clases tomarás el semestre/el año próximo?

    _____

➤➤➤➤➤

4. ¿Qué harás después de graduarte?

_____

5. ¿Qué cosas querrás hacer y ver durante las vacaciones?

_____

6. ¿Qué sueños te gustaría realizar en la vida?

_____

7. ¿Qué harías con un millón de dólares?

_____

J. **Composición.** Write a composition of eight to ten sentences using the future tense to describe what your life will be like in the year 2020. Use the conditional tense to suggest what you would like to be doing at that time.

This vocabulary list contains all the words used in the exercises and introduced in the vocabulary boxes. For nouns of profession and for adjectives, only the masculine forms are given. Note that fundamental vocabulary, such as months, days of the week, and numbers, has not been included.

Conjugation reminders are given for verbs with spelling changes. A note such as **comenzar** (z ➤ c/e) should be read as "z changes to c before e." Stem-changing verbs are indicated as follows: **pensar (e ➤ ie), volver (o ➤ ue), pedir (e ➤ i).** Many irregular forms are given in parentheses.

Abbreviations

d.o.	direct object	*masc.*	masculine
fem.	feminine	*pl.*	plural
i.o.	indirect object	*sing.*	singular
irreg.	irregular		

	a la derecha to the right		**ahora** now
	a la izquierda to the left		**ahora mismo** right now
	a menudo often		**ahorrar** to save
	a propósito by the way	el	**ajedrez** chess
	¿a quién?, ¿a quiénes? whom? *(object)*	el	**ajo** garlic
	a veces sometimes		**al aire libre** open-air
	abajo down, downstairs		**al fondo** in back, at the bottom
el	**abogado** lawyer		**al lado** next door, close by
el	**abrazo** hug	el	**alambre** wire
	abrir to open	el	**albañil** bricklayer
	aburrido bored; boring	el	**albergue juvenil** youth hostel
	acabar de to have just *(done something)*	la	**albóndiga** meatball
	acatarrado with a cold	el	**álbum de sellos/fotos** stamp/photo album
el	**aceite de oliva** olive oil		**alegrarse (de)** to be glad, happy
la	**aceituna** olive	la	**alegría** happiness
	acompañar to go with, accompany		**alemán (alemana)** German
	acordarse (o ➤ ue) (de) to remember	la	**alfombra** rug
	acostarse (o ➤ ue) to go to bed	el	**álgebra** algebra
el	**actor** actor		**algo** something
la	**actriz** actress	el	**algodón** cotton
el	**acuario** aquarium		**alguien** someone, somebody
	administrar to manage, to run		**alguna vez** sometime
	¿adónde? where? (to what place?)		**algunas veces** sometimes
el	**aeropuerto** airport		**alguno (algún), alguna** some
	afeitarse to shave	el	**alimento** food
el	**aficionado** fan (supporter)	el	**alma** *(fem.)* soul, spirit
	afortunado fortunate	el	**almacén** department store
las	**afueras** outskirts; suburbs		**almacenar** to store
la	**agencia de viajes** travel agency	la	**almendra** almond
la	**agenda** appointment book; assignment book		**almorzar (o ➤ ue; z ➤ c/e)** to have lunch
el	**agente de viajes** travel agent	el	**alpinismo** mountain climbing
	agradable pleasant, nice		**alquilar** to rent
	agradecer (agradezco) to thank		**alto** tall
la	**agricultura** agriculture	el	**alumno** student
el	**agua** *(fem.)* water		**amable** friendly

ambicioso ambitious

el **amigo/la amiga por correspondencia**
  pen pal

la **amistad** friendship

amueblado furnished

ancho wide

andar *(irreg.)* to walk

andar en bicicleta to ride a bicycle

el **andén** platform

el **anillo** ring

animarse to cheer up

anoche last night

anteayer day before yesterday

los **anteojos** eyeglasses

antiguo old

antipático unpleasant

la **antropología** anthropology

el **anuncio** ad

añadir to add

el **año pasado** last year

el **año próximo** next year

apagar (g > gu/e) to turn off (an appliance)

el **aparato** appliance

aparecer (aparezco) to appear

el **apartamento** apartment

aplaudir to applaud

aprender (a) to learn (to)

aprender de memoria to memorize

aprobar (o > ue) to pass (an exam)

aprovechar to take advantage

árabe Arab

el **árbol** tree

la **arena** sand

el **arete** earring

el **argumento** plot

armar un lío to raise a fuss, to cause trouble

el **armario** closet

el **arquero** goaltender

el **arquitecto** architect

arreglar to arrange, fix up

arreglarse to get oneself ready, fix up

arriba up, upstairs

el **arroz** rice

el **arte** art

el **artículo** article

artísticamente artistically

asado baked

el **ascensor** elevator

el **asiento** seat

la **asignatura** school subject

asistir (a) to attend (an event); to go (to)

asustarse to get scared

atentamente attentively

el **átlas** atlas

el/la **atleta** athlete

atlético athletic

atrás in back

el **autor** author

el/la **auxiliar de vuelo** flight attendant

la **avenida** avenue

el **avión** airplane

ayudar to help

el **azúcar** sugar

el **bailarín** dancer

bajar to go down(stairs); *(transitive)* to lower, to take down

bajo short

el **baloncesto** basketball

el **banco** bank

la **banda** band

el **banquero** banker

el **banquete** feast

bañarse to take a bath; to bathe (oneself)

el **barco** boat

barrer to sweep

el **barrio** neighborhood

la **basura** trash

el **bebé** baby

el **béisbol** baseball

la **belleza** beauty

el **beso** kiss

la **biblioteca** library

la **bicicleta** bicycle

bilingüe bilingual

la **biografía** biography

la **biología** biology

el **bocadillo** sandwich on roll

la **boda** wedding

el **boleto** ticket

el **bolígrafo** pen, ballpoint pen

la **bolsa** bag; stock market

el **bombón** (*pl.* **los bombones**) candy

bonito pretty

borrar to delete; to erase

el **bosque** forest, woods

el **botiquín** medicine cabinet; first-aid kit

bronceado suntanned

bucear to go scuba diving

Buen provecho. Enjoy your meal.

la **bufanda** scarf

buscar (c > qu/e) to look for

el **caballo** horse

caber *(irreg.)* to fit

caer *(irreg.)* to fall

caerse to fall down

el **café** coffee; café

la **cafetería** cafeteria

la **caja** box

el **cajón** crate, drawer

los **calcetines** socks *(Spain)*

la **calculadora** calculator

calmarse to calm down

la **cama** bed

la **cámara** camera

el **camarón** shrimp

el **cambio** change

caminar to walk

la **caminata** walk, hike

la **camisa** shirt

la **camiseta** T-shirt

el **campo** country(side)

el **campo de juego** playing field

cansado tired

cansarse to get tired

cantar to sing
la capital capital city
el capítulo chapter
la caridad charity
cariñoso loving, affectionate
la carne meat
la carnicería butcher shop
la carrera course of study, profession
la carretera highway
el carro car
la carta letter
el cartel poster
la cartera wallet; handbag
casarse (con) to get married (to)
el casete cassette
casi almost
casualidad: ¡Qué casualidad! What a coincidence!
el catarro cold (illness)
la catedral cathedral
celebrar to celebrate
cenar to have dinner
el centro downtown; center of the city
el centro comercial shopping mall
cepillarse el pelo/los dientes to brush one's
    hair/teeth
cercano nearby
el cereal cereal
la cereza cherry
cerrar (e ➢ ie) to close
el césped lawn; grass
el champú shampoo
la chaqueta jacket
el cheque check
la chequera checkbook
chino Chinese
el chiste joke
la chuleta de ternera veal chop
el ciclismo bicycle riding
la ciencia science; knowledge
la ciencia ficción science fiction
las ciencias science
las ciencias de medio ambiente environmental sciences
el científico scientist
el cine movie theater; movies
la cinta tape (audio)
el cinturón belt
el circo circus
el clarinete clarinet
claro (que) of course
clásico classical
el cliente customer
la clínica clinic
el coche car
el coche todo terreno jeep
cocinar to cook
el cocinero chef; cook
coger (g ➢ j/a,o) to catch
colaborar to contribute; to collaborate
el colegio preescolar nursery school
colgar (o ➢ ue; g ➢ gu/e) to hang
el collar necklace
colocar (c ➢ qu/e) to put, place
el comedor dining room; cafeteria

comenzar (e ➢ ie; z ➢ c/e) to begin
comer to eat
cómico funny
la comida food; meal
comilón gluttonous
el comité committee
¿cómo? how?; what?
cómodo comfortable
el compañero classmate
la compañía company
compartir to share
completamente completely
complicado complicated
el compositor composer
comprar to buy
comprensivo understanding
la computadora computer
la comunidad community
el concierto concert
concluir (concluyo) to finish; to deduce
conducir (conduzco) to drive
la conferencia lecture
la confitería tea room
congelado frozen
el congreso congress; convention
conocer (conozco) to know
conocido famous
conseguir (e ➢ i; gu ➢ g/a,o) to get, to acquire;
    to manage to (with infinitive)
los consejos advice
constante constant, steady
construir (construyo) to build
el consultorio doctor's office
la contabilidad accounting
el contable accountant
contar (o ➢ ue) to count; to tell
contar con to count/rely on
continuar (continúo) to continue
convencer (c ➢ z/a,o) to convince
la corbata necktie
el correo mail; post office
el correo electrónico e-mail
correr to run
cortar to cut
cortarse el pelo to cut one's hair
cortés polite, courteous
la cortina curtain
la costa seashore, coast
costar (o ➢ ue) to cost
costoso expensive, costly
la costumbre custom
crear una carpeta to create a file
crecer (crezco) to grow
creer to believe; to think
el cristal glass
el cuadro picture, painting
¿cuál?, ¿cuáles? which one(s)?
cualquier(a) any
¿cuándo? when?
¿cuánto(a)? how much?
¿cuántos(as)? how many?
el cuarto room
la cucharadita teaspoon

la **cuenta** bill
el **cuero** leather
cuidadoso careful
cuidar (a/de) to take care (of)
cultivar to grow
cumplido accomplished
la **cuñada** sister-in-law
el **cuñado** brother-in-law
cursar to take a course
el **cursor** cursor

dar *(irreg.)* to give
dar a to face
dar un paseo to take a walk
dar una película to show a movie
los **datos** information; data; facts
de alguna manera/de algún modo somehow, in some way
de cuadros checked
¿de dónde? from where?
de ida y vuelta round-trip
de ninguna manera/de ningún modo in no way
¿de quién?, ¿de quiénes? whose?
de rayas striped
de vez en cuando from time to time
debajo de under, beneath
deber should, ought to
débil weak
la **debilidad** weakness
decidir to decide
decir *(irreg.)* to say, tell
la **decoración de escaparates** window dressing
decorar to decorate
dedicado dedicated
dedicarse (c ➤ qu/e) (a) to devote oneself (to)
dejar to leave; to let, allow
dejar de to stop *(doing something)*
delante (de) in front (of)
delgado thin
demostrar (o ➤ ue) to show; to prove
el/la **dentista** dentist
el **departamento** department
el **deporte** sport
desaparecer (desaparezco) to disappear
desarrollar to develop
desayunarse to have breakfast
descansado rested
descansar to rest
descompuesto broken; out of order
desconcertado upset
descuidado careless
desear to want; to wish
el **desfile** parade
despacio slow
despedir (e ➤ i) to send away, dismiss; to fire
despedirse (de) to say good-bye (to)
el **despegue** takeoff (airplane)
despertarse (e ➤ ie) to wake up
destruir (destruyo) to destroy
detrás (de) behind
devolver (o ➤ ue) to return, give something back

dibujar to draw
los **dibujos animados** cartoons
dictar una conferencia to give a lecture
difícil difficult
la **dificultad** difficulty
diligente diligent; industrious
el **dinero** money
la **dirección** address
directo direct
el **director de cine** movie director
el **director de orquesta** orchestra conductor
dirigir (g ➤ j/a,o) to conduct *(orchestra);* to direct
el **disco compacto** compact disk
la **discoteca** dance club, discotheque
discreto discreet, tactful
discutir to argue, discuss heatedly
el **disquete** diskette
divertido amusing
divertirse (e ➤ ie) to have fun, a good time
el **documento** document, official paper
el **dólar** dollar
doler (o ➤ ue) *(with i.o. pronoun)* to hurt, ache
¿dónde? where? (at what place?)
dormir (o ➤ ue) to sleep
dormir la siesta to take a nap
dormirse to fall asleep
el **dormitorio** bedroom
ducharse to take a shower
dudar to doubt
el **dueño** owner
dulce sweet
durante during

echar un brindis to toast *(at a ceremony)*
la **economía** economy; economics
económico economical
la **edad** age
el **edificio** building
egoísta selfish
el **ejercicio aeróbico** aerobic exercise
el **elefante** elephant
la **elegancia** elegance
elegante elegant
elegir (e ➤ i; g ➤ j/a,o) to elect
la **embajada** embassy
emocionado excited
emocionarse to get excited
empezar (e ➤ ie; z ➤ c/e) to begin
el **empleado** employee
la **empresa** company, firm
en casa at home
en este momento at this moment
en otra oportunidad at some other time
en realidad in fact; actually
en seguida right away
en voz alta aloud
en/por algún lado/sitio/lugar somewhere
en/por alguna parte somewhere
en/por ningún lado/sitio/lugar nowhere
en/por ninguna parte nowhere
en punto on the dot

en tren/avión by train/plane
enamorarse (de) to fall in love (with)
encantador charming, delightful
encantarle a alguien to love something
encima de on, upon, on top of
encontrar (o ➢ ue) to find
enfadado angry
enfadarse to get angry
enfermarse to get sick
enfermo sick, ill
enfrente opposite, across
enojarse to get angry
la **ensalada** salad
la **ensaladilla rusa** potato salad
el **ensayo** essay
enseñar to teach; to show
ensuciarse to get dirty
entender (e ➢ ie) to understand
entonces then
la **entrada** ticket *(for a show or event)*
entre between, among
entregar (g ➢ gu/e) to hand in, over
los **entremeses** hors d'oeuvres
entusiasmado excited, enthused
enviar (envío) to send
envolver (o ➢ ue) to wrap *(something)*
el **equipaje** luggage
el **equipo** team
la **equitación** horseback riding
la **escalera mecánica** escalator
el **escalope** boneless veal cutlet
escocés (escocesa) Scottish
escoger (g ➢ j/a,o) to choose, select
el **escondite** hide-and-seek
el **escritor** writer
el **escritorio** desk
escuchar to listen
el **escultor** sculptor
la **escultura** sculpture
español (española) Spanish
esparcir (c ➢ z/a,o) to scatter *(something)*
el **espectáculo** show
la **esperanza** hope
esperar to wait; to expect; to hope
la **esposa** wife
el **esposo** husband
el **esquí** ski, skiing
esquiar (esquío) to ski
establecer (establezco) to establish
la **estación de invierno** winter resort
la **estación de tren** train station
el **estacionamiento** parking spot, parking lot
estacionar to park
el **estadio** stadium
la **estadística** statistics
estadounidense from/of the United States
la **estantería** bookcase
estar acatarrado to have a cold
estar de acuerdo to agree
estar de vacaciones to be on vacation
estar de viaje to be traveling
estar de vuelta to be back
estar en oferta to be on sale

estar frito to be all washed up, done for
estar hecho un asco to be filthy, disgusting *(to look at)*
estar resfriado to have a cold
este... umm . . . *(stall in speaking)*
el **estéreo** stereo
el **estómago** stomach
estornudar to sneeze
la **estrella** star
estudiar para *(+ profession)* to study to be a
el **estudio** study
el **examen** exam, test
la **excursión** outing, trip
exigirle (g ➢ j/a,o) algo a alguien to demand something of someone
el **experimento** experiment
explicar (c ➢ qu/e) to explain
exportar to export
la **exposición** exhibit
expresar to express
extrañarle a alguien to surprise someone
extranjero foreign

la **fabada asturiana** Asturian stew *(Spain)*
la **fábrica** factory
fácil easy
facturar to check
faltarle a alguien to be missing something, not to have
familiar family *(adjective)*
la **farmacia** pharmacy, drugstore
fascinarle a alguien to be fascinated by, interested in
la **fecha** date
feliz happy
el **fichero** filing cabinet
la **fiesta** party
finalmente finally
el **fin de semana** weekend
la **finca** farm, ranch
la **física** physics
flaco skinny
el **flamenco** flamenco *(dance)*
el **flan** custard
la **flauta** flute
flojo lazy
la **flor** flower
la **florería** flower shop
folklórico folk, traditional
la **formación** training, education
formal serious; reliable
formidable impressive
la **foto** photo
fotocopiar to photocopy
la **fotografía** photograph
el **fotógrafo** photographer
frecuentemente frequently
el **freno** brake
frente a across from, facing
fresco fresh
frito fried; washed up, in a bad way *(past participle freír)*

	fuerte strong; hard *(force)*		**hacer sol** to be sunny
la	**función** show, performance		**hacer travesuras** to play tricks
	funcionar to work, function *(machine)*		**hacer turismo** to go touring, see the sights
el	**fundador** founder		**hacer un viaje** to take a trip
	fundar to found, establish		**hacerle falta a alguien** to need something
el	**fútbol** soccer		**hacerse** to become
el	**fútbol americano** football		**hacerse daño** to hurt oneself
		la	**hacienda** ranch
		el	**hambre** *(fem.)* hunger
las	**gafas** eyeglasses	la	**hamburguesa** hamburger
la	**galleta** cookie; cracker		**hasta** even; until
el	**ganado** livestock		**hay** there is; there are *(from **haber**)*
	ganar to earn; to win		**hecho** done, made *(past participle **hacer**)*
el	**garaje** garage		**hecho: muy hecho/poco hecho**
el	**gato** cat		overcooked/undercooked *(meat)*
la	**gaveta** drawer	la	**heladería** ice-cream store
el	**gazpacho** cold tomato soup *(Spain)*		**hermoso** beautiful
los	**gemelos** twins; binoculars; cuff links	la	**herramienta** tool
	generalmente generally, usually	el	**higo** fig
la	**generosidad** generosity	la	**historia** history; story
	generoso generous	la	**hoja** leaf
	genial brilliant	el	**hombre de negocios** businessman
la	**gente** people		**honesto** decent; honest
el	**gentío** crowd	el	**horario** schedule; timetable
el	**gerente** manager	el	**horno** oven
la	**gimnasia** gymnastics		**horrible** horrible, terrible
el	**globo** balloon		**horrorizarse** (z ≻ c/e) to be horrified
el	**gobierno** government	el	**hospital** hospital
el	**gol** goal *(sports)*	la	**hostelería** hotel management
	gordo fat	el	**hotel** hotel
el	**gorro** cap		**huir (huyo)** to flee
	gracioso witty; amusing		
el	**grado** degree *(temperature)*		
la	**gramática** grammar		**idealista** idealistic
	grande big	el	**idioma** language
	grave serious	la	**iglesia** church
	gritar to shout, yell	la	**igualdad** equality
el	**guante** glove		**impaciente** impatient
	guapo handsome, good-looking	el	**impermeable** raincoat
	guardar to keep, put away		**importarle a alguien** to care about something;
	guardar cama to stay in bed		to mind
	guardar los datos to keep, save data		**impresionar** to impress
	gustarle a alguien to like	la	**impresora** printer
			incluir (incluyo) to include
		el	**informe** report
	haber *(irreg.)* to have *(auxiliary verb)*	el	**ingeniero** engineer
la	**habitación** room		**inglés (inglesa)** English
el	**habla** speech		**inolvidable** unforgettable
	hace *(+ expression of time + present tense)* for		**insistir en** to insist on
	(+ time expression)		**instalarse** to get settled in
	hace *(+ expression of time + preterit tense)* ago	las	**instrucciones** directions, instructions
	hacer *(irreg.)* to do; to make		**intelectual** intellectual
	hacer la cama to make the bed		**inteligente** intelligent, smart
	hacer clic del ratón to click on the mouse		**interesarle a alguien** to be interested in
	hacer cola to stand in line	el	**intérprete** interpreter
	hacer unas diligencias to run errands		**inútil** useless
	hacer ejercicio to exercise	el	**invitado** guest
	hacer una excursión to go on an outing		**invitar (a)** to invite (to)
	hacer investigaciones to do research		**ir** *(irreg.)* to go
	hacer juego con to match		**ir de compras** to go shopping
	hacer las paces to make up		**irlandés (irlandesa)** Irish
	hacer planes to make plans		**irse** to go away
	hacer reventar to burst		**italiano** Italian

	jamás never			**llover (o ➤ ue)** to rain
el	**jamón** ham			**llover a cántaros** to rain cats and dogs, rain hard
	japonés (japonesa) Japanese			**lo antes posible** as soon as possible
el	**jarabe para la tos** cough syrup		la	**luz** light
el	**jardín botánico** botanic garden			
el	**jefe** boss			
el	**jefe de estado** head of state		el	**maestro** teacher
el	**jerez** sherry		el	**maíz** corn
la	**joyería** jewelry store		el	**malcriado** brat
el	**juego** game		la	**maleta** suitcase
el	**jugador** player		las	**mallas** tights
	jugar (u ➤ ue; g ➤ gu/e) (a) to play *(a sport or game)*			**mandar** to send
			el	**mandato** order, command
el	**juguete** toy			**manejar** to drive
	juntos together		la	**manga** sleeve
la	**juventud** youth		la	**manzana** apple
			el	**mapa** map
				maquillarse to put on makeup
el	**laboratorio de lenguas** language laboratory		el	**mar** sea, ocean
el	**ladrón** thief			**maravilloso** wonderful
la	**lámpara** lamp		la	**marca** make, brand
la	**lana** wool			**marcar (c ➤ qu/e) un gol** to score a goal
la	**langosta** lobster		el	**marido** husband
el	**lápiz** pencil		la	**materia** subject *(school)*
	largo long			**matricularse** to get enrolled
la	**lástima** pity, shame		el	**mecánico** mechanic
el	**lavaplatos** dishwasher			**media hora** half an hour
	lavar to wash		las	**medias** socks; stockings *(Spain)*
	lavarse to wash up		el	**médico** doctor
	lavarse la cabeza/el pelo to wash one's hair			**medio muerto** half-dead
la	**leche** milk		el	**membrillo** quince
	leer to read		el	**mensaje** message
la	**legumbre** vegetable			**mentir (e ➤ ie)** to lie
la	**lengua** language			**merendar (e ➤ ie)** to have an afternoon snack
el	**lente de contacto** contact lens		la	**merluza** hake, cod
	levantar to raise		la	**mermelada** jam, marmalade
	levantarse to get up			**meter** to put inside
la	**libertad** freedom, liberty		la	**mezcla** mixture
la	**librería** bookstore			**mezclar** to mix
el	**libro de cocina** cookbook		la	**miel** honey
el	**libro de consulta** reference book			**mientras** while
el	**libro de texto** textbook			**mimado** spoiled
la	**licencia de manejar** driver's license			**mirar** to look at, watch
la	**liga mayor** major league		la	**mochila** backpack
	ligero light		el	**módem** modem
el	**limón** lemon		la	**modista** dressmaker
la	**limonada** lemonade			**molestar** to annoy; to bother
el	**limpiaparabrisas** windshield wiper			**molestarse** to get annoyed
	limpiar to clean			**molesto** annoying; bothersome
	limpiarse los dientes to brush one's teeth		la	**moneda** coin; currency
	listo smart, clever; ready		el	**monedero** coin/change purse
la	**literatura** literature			**mono** cute, adorable
	llamar to call		la	**montaña** mountain
	llamar a la puerta to knock at the door			**montar a caballo** to go horseback riding
la	**llave** key			**montar en bicicleta** to ride a bicycle
	llegar (g ➤ gu/e) to arrive, come			**moreno** dark-haired
	llegar a to get to; to succeed in			**morir(se) (o ➤ ue)** to die
	llegar a ser to become			**morirse de hambre** to die of hunger
	llenar to fill			**mostrar (o ➤ ue)** to show
	llevar to carry; to wear; to take *(somebody somewhere)*		la	**motocicleta** motorcycle
				mover (o ➤ ue) to move
	llevar una vida sana to lead a healthy life		la	**moza** waitress
	llorar to cry			**muchas veces** often

la	muchedumbre crowd			ojalá I hope; here's hoping; let's hope
	mudarse to move (change residence)		la	ola wave
el	mueble piece of furniture		el	olivo olive tree
los	muebles furniture		la	ópera opera
la	mujer de negocios businesswoman			optimista optimistic
el	museo museum			ordenar to straighten up
la	música music		la	organización organization
el	músico musician			organizar (z ➤ c/e) to straighten; to put in order
				orgulloso proud
	nacer (nazco) to be born		el	origen background, origin
la	nacionalidad nationality		el	oro gold
	nada nothing		la	orquesta orchestra
	nadar to swim			oscuro dark
	nadie nobody			otra vez again
los	naipes playing cards			
la	naranja orange			paciente patient
la	nariz nose			pagar (g ➤ gu/e) to pay
la	nata batida whipped cream		el	país country
la	naturaleza nature		el	paisaje landscape
	navegar (g ➤ gu/e) to sail		el	pájaro bird
	navegar en el web to surf on the web			pálido pale
la	Navidad Christmas		el	pan bread
	necesario necessary		el	pan tostado toast
	necesitar to need		la	panadería bakery
	nevar (e ➤ ie) to snow		la	pantalla screen (of computer, TV set)
	ni, ni siquiera not even		el	pañuelo de papel tissue
	ni... ni... neither . . . nor		la	papa potato
la	niebla fog		la	papelera wastepaper basket
la	nieta granddaughter		la	papelería stationery store
el	nieto grandson		el	paquete package
los	nietos grandchildren		el	par pair
	ninguno (ningún), ninguna no, not a			¿para qué? for what purpose?
el	niñero babysitter		el	paraguas umbrella
	No puedo más. I can't stand it anymore.			parar to stop
	norteamericano North American			parecer (parezco) to seem
las	notas grades			parecerle a alguien to think of
las	noticias news		la	pared wall
la	novela policíaca detective novel		la	pareja couple
la	novia girlfriend; bride		el	pariente relative (family)
el	noviazgo courtship		el	parque de atracciones amusement park
el	novio boyfriend; groom		el	parque zoológico zoo
los	novios bride and groom; newlyweds			pasado rotten, overripe (fruit)
la	nube cloud		el	pasajero passenger
	nublado cloudy			pasar to happen; spend time
el	número size (shoe)			pasar la aspiradora to vacuum
el	número de teléfono telephone number			pasear to walk around; to take for a walk
	nunca never			pasearse to walk around
	nunca más never again		el	pastel pastry; pie
	nutritivo nourishing, nutritious		el	pastelero pastry chef
			el	pastor minister
	o or			patinar to skate
	o... o... either . . . or			patinar sobre hielo to ice skate
la	obra maestra masterpiece			pedir (e ➤ i) to ask for; to order
la	obra (de teatro) play			pedir prestado to borrow
	ocurrir to happen			pegar (g ➤ gu/e) to hit
	ocurrírsele a alguien to dawn on/occur to someone			peinarse to comb one's hair
	ofenderse to get insulted, offended		el	peine comb
la	ofimática office technology		la	película film
	ofrecer (ofrezco) to offer			peligroso dangerous
	oír (irreg.) to hear			pelirrojo redheaded
			la	peluquería beauty salon; barber shop
			el	pendiente earring

pensar (e ➤ ie) (en; de) to think (about; of)
pensar (+ infinitive) to intend to
pequeño small
perder (e ➤ ie) to lose; to miss (train, etc.); to waste (time)
la perfección perfection
perfeccionar to improve, brush up
perfectamente perfectly
la perfumería perfume store
el periódico newspaper
el periodista journalist, reporter
la perla pearl
el permiso permission
el perro dog
pertenecer (pertenezco) to belong
el pescado fish (caught)
pesimista pessimistic
petroquímico petrochemical
el pez fish (live)
picar (c ➤ qu/e) to chop
el picazón insect bite
el pie foot
la piñata decorated papier-maché or ceramic party container full of sweets
el pintor painter
la pintura painting
la piscina swimming pool
el piso floor
la pista de correr running track
la pizarra chalkboard
planear to plan
la planificación urbana urban planning
el plástico plastic
la plata money; silver
el plátano banana
platicar (c ➤ qu/e) to chat
el plato dish (food)
la playa beach
la plaza square
la pluma pen
poder (o ➤ ue; irreg.) to be able, can
el poema poem
la poesía poetry
polaco Polish
la poliomielitis polio
la política politics
el político politician
político political
el pollo al chilindrón chicken with tomatoes and peppers
poner (irreg.) to put
poner al día to bring up to date
poner la mesa to set the table
poner en orden to straighten up
ponerse (+ article of clothing) to put on
ponerse (+ adjective) to become
ponerse en forma to get into shape
ponerse rojo to blush
por algún lado somewhere
por algún sitio somewhere
por ejemplo for example
por eso therefore, that's why
por fin finally

por ningún lado nowhere
por ningún sitio nowhere
¿por qué? why?
porque because
por supuesto of course
por todas partes everywhere
portátil portable
el portero goaltender
portugués (portuguesa) Portuguese
posible possible
posiblemente possibly
el postre dessert
practicar (c ➤ qu/e) to practice
el precio price
precioso lovely, pretty
el preescolar nursery school
preferir (e ➤ ie) to prefer
preocupado worried
preocuparse to worry
preparar to prepare, make
el presidente president
prestar to lend, loan
los primos cousins
el principio beginning
probar (o ➤ ue) to try; to taste
probarse to try on
producir (produzco) to produce
el producto product
profundo deep
el programa program
el programador de computadoras computer programmer
prohibir to forbid, prohibit
el pronóstico (meteorológico) weather forecast
pronunciar to pronounce
la propina tip
próspero prosperous
el proyecto project
la prueba quiz
la psicología psychology
el psicólogo psychologist
el público audience
la puerta gate; door
el puesto stand, small shop; position (job)
pulsar to click (a mouse)
la pulsera bracelet

¿qué? what?
quedar to be (located); to remain, be left
quedar en to agree to
quedarle a alguien to have something left
quedarse to remain, stay
los quehaceres domésticos household chores
quemarse to burn oneself
querer (e ➤ ie; irreg.) to want; to love
querer decir to mean
el queso cheese
¿quién?, ¿quiénes? who (subject)
la química chemistry
el quiosco newsstand
quitar el corazón to core (fruit)

quitar la mesa to clear the table
quitarle algo a alguien to take something away
    from someone
quitarse (+ *article of clothing*) to take off
quizás maybe, perhaps

la   radio radio
el   ramo de flores bouquet
el   rancho ranch
la   raqueta de tenis tennis racquet
    raro strange
el   rascacielos skyscraper
el   rato while
el   ratón mouse (*animal; computer accessory*)
    realista realistic
    realmente really
la   receta recipe
    recibir to receive
    recién llegado recently, newly arrived
el   recinto universitario college campus
    recoger (g ≻ j/a,o) to gather; to pick up
    recomendar (e ≻ ie) to recommend
    reconocer (reconozco) to recognize
    recordar (o ≻ ue) to remember
    recordarle a alguien to remind someone
el   recuerdo souvenir
    referir (e ≻ ie) to refer
el   refrán proverb
los   refrescos refreshments
    regalar to give (as a gift)
el   regalo gift
    regar (e ≻ ie) to water
    regresar to return, go back
    reírse (*irreg.*) to laugh
las   relaciones públicas public relations
    relajarse to relax
el   reloj watch, clock
    reparar to repair
    repasar to review
    repetir (e ≻ i) to repeat; to have a second helping
    (*of food*)
    resbaloso slippery
la   reservación reservation
la   residencia dormitory
    resolver (o ≻ ue) to solve; to resolve
    responsable reliable
el   retraso delay
la   reunión meeting; reunion
    reunirse (reúno) (con) to get together (with)
la   revista de modas fashion magazine
    rico rich; delicious
    ridículo ridiculous
    robarle algo a alguien to steal something from
    someone
    romántico romantic
    romper to break
    romperse (+ *part of body*) to break; (+ *article of*
    clothing) to tear
la   ropa interior underwear
la   rosa rose
    rubio blonde
el   ruido noise

    ruidoso noisy
    ruso Russian

    saber (*irreg.*) to know
el   sabor flavor, taste
    sabroso tasty, delicious
el   sacapuntas pencil sharpener
    sacar (c ≻ qu/e) to take out
    sacar buenas notas to get good grades
    sacar entradas/billetes to get tickets
    sacar fotos to take photos
    sacudir el polvo to dust
la   sal salt
    salado salty
    salir (salgo) to go out, leave
    salir bien/mal en un examen to do well/poorly
    on an exam
    salírsele un novio to get a boyfriend
el   salmón salmon
el   salón concert hall; classroom
la   salsa picante hot/spicy sauce
la   salud health
el   sándwich sandwich
    sano healthy, healthful
    secar (c ≻ qu/e) to dry
el   secretario secretary
la   seda silk
    seguir (e ≻ i; gu ≻ g/a,o) to follow; to
    continue
    segundo second
la   seguridad safety; security
el   sello stamp
el   semestre semester
el   seminario seminar
la   sencillez simplicity
    sensible sensitive
    sentarse (e ≻ ie) to sit down
el   sentimiento feeling, emotion
    sentir (e ≻ ie) to be sorry (*with lo: lo siento*);
    to regret
    sentirse to feel
la   serie series
    serio serious
los   servicios facilities, amenities
la   servilleta napkin
    servir (e ≻ i) to serve
    si if
    siempre always
la   sierra mountains, mountain range
    simpático nice, pleasant
    sincero sincere
la   sinfonía symphony
el   sistema system
la   situación situation
la   sobremesa after-dinner chat
la   sobrina niece
el   sobrino nephew
    solucionar problemas to solve problems
    sonar (o ≻ ue) el teléfono to ring
    soñar (o ≻ ue) (con) to dream (of/about)
la   sopa de gallina chicken soup
    sorprender to surprise

el   **sótano** basement
      subir to go up; to get on; *(transitive)* to raise; to take up
el   **subterráneo (subte)** subway *(Argentina)*
la   **sucursal** branch *(of business)*
la   **suegra** mother-in-law
el   **suegro** father-in-law
la   **suerte** luck
el   **suéter** sweater
      sufrir to suffer
      sugerir (e ≻ ie) to suggest
      suizo Swiss
      sumamente extremely
el   **supermercado** supermarket

      talentoso talented
la   **talla** size *(garments)*
el   **tamaño** size; shoe size
      también also, too
      tampoco neither, not either
la   **taquilla** box office
      tardar en to delay in, be long in
      tarde late
la   **tarea** homework
la   **tarjeta** card
la   **tarjeta de crédito** credit card
la   **tarjeta de embarque** boarding pass
la   **tarjeta postal** postcard
la   **tarta** tart
el   **té** tea
el   **teatro** theater
      teclear to type
el   **técnico** manager, trainer
la   **tecnología** technology
la   **tele** TV
la   **telenovela** TV serial, soap opera
el   **telesquí** ski lift
la   **televisión** television
el   **televisor** television set
el   **tema** topic
el   **templo** temple
      tener *(irreg.)* to have
      tener... años to be . . . years old
      tener catarro to have a cold
      tener éxito to be successful
      tener ganas (de) to feel like
      tener hambre to be hungry
      tener miedo (de) to be afraid (of)
      tener prisa to be in a hurry
      tener que to have to
      tener razón to be right
      tener sed to be thirsty
      tener sueño to be sleepy
      tener suerte to be lucky
el   **tenis** tennis
      terminar to finish; to end
      terminar de to stop *(doing something)*
el   **tiempo** time; weather
la   **tienda de comestibles** grocery store
la   **tienda de discos** record store
la   **tienda de recuerdos** souvenir shop
la   **tienda de videos** video store

las   **tijeras** scissors
la   **timidez** shyness
      tímido shy
la   **tintorería** dry cleaner *(shop)*
los   **tíos** aunt and uncle
      típico typical
      tirar to throw; to throw out/away
el   **título** title
la   **toalla** towel
el   **tocadiscos** record player; CD player
      tocar (c ≻ qu/e) to play *(instrument)*
      tocarle a alguien to be someone's turn
      todavía still; **todavía no** not yet
      todo el día all day
      tomar apuntes to take notes
      tomar fotos to take pictures
      tomar una resolución to make a resolution
el   **tomate** tomato
      tonto silly, stupid
la   **torre** tower
la   **torta** cake
la   **tortilla** omelet *(Spain)*
      toser to cough
      totalmente completely, totally
      trabajador hard-working
      trabajar to work
      trabajar de niñera to babysit
      trabajar en parejas to work in pairs
la   **tradición** tradition
      tradicional traditional
      traducir (traduzco) to translate
      traer *(irreg.)* to bring
el   **traje de baño** swimsuit
el   **traje regional** regional costume
los   **trámites** procedures
      tranquilizarse (z ≻ c/e) to calm down
      tratar de to try to
      travieso mischievous
el   **tren de cercanías** commuter train
el   **trigo** wheat
la   **trompeta** trumpet
el   **tronco: dormir como un tronco** to sleep soundly/like a log
      trotar to jog, go jogging
el   **tulipán** tulip
el/la **turista** tourist

      últimamente lately
      último last
      único only; unique
      unido close, united
la   **unión** union
la   **universidad** university
      universitario university *(adjective)*
      usar to use; to wear
      útil useful
los   **útiles de escuela** school supplies
la   **uva** grape

      vaciar (vacío) to empty
      vacío empty

	valer (valgo) to be worth		**visitar** to visit
	valiente brave	la	**vitamina** vitamin
el	**vaso** glass		**vivir** to live
el	**vegetal** vegetable	el	**vólibol** volleyball
la	**vela** candle		**volver (o ➢ ue)** to return, go/come back
el	**velero** sailboat		**volver a** + *infinitive* to do something again
	vencer (venzo) to conquer; to defeat		**volverse** (+ *adjective*) to become
el	**vendedor** salesperson		**volverse loco** to go/become crazy
	vender to sell	la	**voz** voice
	venir *(irreg.)* to come		
	ver *(irreg.)* to see		
	verdaderamente truly, really	el	**web** web
	vestirse (e ➢ i) to dress, get dressed	el	**windsurfing** windsurfing *(with hacer)*
el	**veterinario** veterinarian		
	viajar to travel		
el	**viaje de negocios** business trip		**ya** already, now
la	**vida** life		**ya no** no longer
la	**videocasetera** videocassette player	la	**yema** egg yolk
la	**videocinta** videotape	el	**yoga** yoga *(exercise)*
el	**videojuego** video game		
el	**villancico** Christmas carol		
el	**violín** violin	la	**zapatilla** slipper

INDEX